OTHERWORLD NORTH EAST

*This book is dedicated to the efforts of all those – living and dead –
who helped with field research.*

Bamburgh Castle on the Northumberland coast, around 1890.

OTHERWORLD NORTH EAST

Ghosts and Hauntings Explored

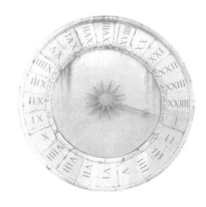

Tony Liddell

Tyne Bridge Publishing

Acknowledgments

Huge thanks to the Otherworld North East team for their invaluable help over the last year – Sarah Clive, Danny Jones, Paul Roberts, Kev Grey, Janet Dodds, Barry Coates, Jill Armstrong, Glen Clough, Dave Bates, Guy Ross, Dean Maynard, Jess Kemp and Marc Johnstone. Thanks also to UK Ghost Investigators, Team Maynard, TAPS (The Answers People Seek) and of course Ghost Haunted. Many thanks to all the guests and volunteers who took part in the investigation, especially Charlotte Lee from Cheshire.

Thanks and gratitude to all the owners, custodians, staff and ground-staff who have aided in, and allowed the investigations of the properties in the Case Studies. Without exception their help and co-operation proved invaluable.

Special thanks must go to Glen Clough for his help on the Marsden Grotto and The House content, and to Suzanne McKay for her input on the Schooner Hotel section; to Ken Smith for his help with Chillingham Castle; to Sarah Clive, Paul McDonald and Trevor Brown for allowing their photographs to be reproduced in the book; to Paul Sandbach and Gordon Teasdale for their help in the early stages of the book and to Heidi Graham, Alan Smallwood, Dean Maynard and Danny Jones, without whose influence I'd probably never had started paranormal investigation in the first place (yes, you're to blame!). Thanks must also go to my friends and family who have supported and helped me during the investigations and writing, and for those who provided timely distractions when I thought if I wrote one more word I'd go insane!

Thanks must also go to those who have given independent views on some of the photographic anomalies and technical details over the last year, including Mike, Christie, Andy, Karl, Caroline, David, Rae and Sarah Hutchinson.

And last but definitely not least, thanks to Tyne Bridge Publishing's Anna Flowers, Vanessa Histon and Shawn Fairless, without whom you definitely wouldn't be holding this book in your hands!

Photographs of investigations ©Tony Liddell, unless otherwise indicated; all other illustrations are from the collections of Newcastle Libraries unless otherwise indicated.

Cover design by Kemi Olusoga.
Cover photograph of Ravensworth Castle (also page 127) by Keith Liddell.

The views expressed in this book are solely the views of the author and do not represent the views of Newcastle City Council.

Otherworld North East ©Tony Liddell 2004

ISBN: 1857951123

Published by City of Newcastle upon Tyne
Education & Libraries Directorate
Newcastle Libraries, Information and Lifelong Learning Service
Tyne Bridge Publishing, 2004

www.tynebridgepublishing.co.uk

Printed by Elanders Hindson, UK

CONTENTS

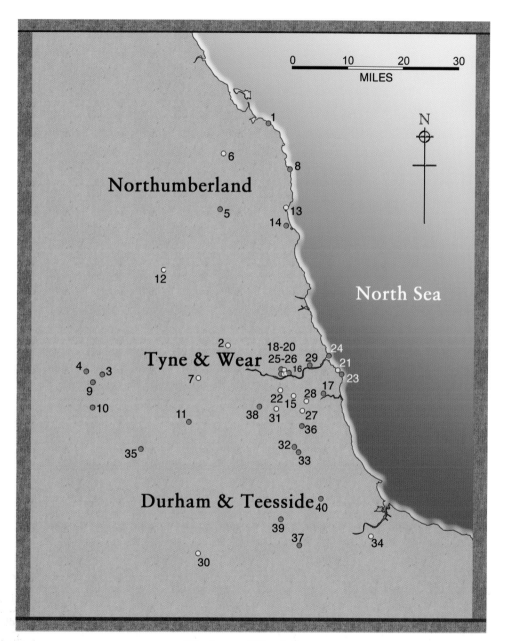

The haunted North East

The Garrison Room at Newcastle Keep, wired up and ready for investigation.

WELCOME TO OTHERWORLD NORTH EAST

Twelve months ago I was asked an amusing question: 'Have you ever come across anything more scary than a football supporter on the losing side?' At the time my glib reply was 'Newcastle or Sunderland supporter?', but if asked that same question now, my immediate and honest response would be 'Oooh yes ...'

With eight years of field archaeology under my belt and what I hope is a rational and rather sceptical mind, I started researching *Otherworld North East*'s tales of the paranormal expecting to find nothing, but hoping to find more than I expected. The overnight vigils were very different from what I was used to. As an archaeologist I usually only had access to sites when they required excavating: now I had access for eight hours at a time, sometimes unlimited, at night – in the dark. It was like being a detective of the past, searching for clues in the environment, or memories in the walls, rather than in the sometimes equally ephemeral archaeological deposits of times past.

Having a good team was a must, and I found what I was looking for. Being invited to investigations by other teams helped too, as each team has its own ways and methods and I'm always eager to learn.

So what was found in a year of research? In this book you will find 40 tales of the supernatural to whet your appetite – 16 of them are case studies. I make no claims, except that all results are honest and as we found them, as are the photographs you'll see. All that remains is for you to judge the evidence and make up your own mind, which is all any of us can truly do...

Tony Liddell, August 2004

Paranormal investigator Tony Liddell heads into the unknown.

AN OPEN MIND?

In the religious and superstitious times between the 16th and 19th centuries, belief in the supernatural was widespread across the country. The idea that ghosts and ghouls waited hungrily in the shadows was commonplace, and tales of hauntings and spiritual activity that ranged from the bizarre to the mundane were rife.

However, as society looked increasingly to science to explain the world, people who had supernatural experiences (or investigated them) were subject to ridicule.

Only recently have paranormal investigators begun to shake off their reputation of eccentricity. With the popularity of television shows such as Living TV's *Most Haunted* more

and more people are willing to come forward with accounts of their experiences, or are at least inclined to keep an open mind.

But how haunted is the North East? Steeped in legend and with a rich history that still leaves its mark on the landscape, the area should have a ghost in every corner, especially if you go by what American poet, Henry Wadsworth Longfellow, had to say in *Haunted Houses* in 1858:

All houses wherein men have lived and died
Are haunted houses. Through the open doors
The harmless phantoms on their errands glide,
With feet that make no sound upon the floors.

We meet them at the door-way, on the stair,
Along the passages they come and go,
Impalpable impressions on the air,
A sense of something moving to and fro.

The words 'paranormal investigator' might make you think of the 1980s film, *Ghostbusters*, or the old Hammer Horror movies. The role is not one usually associated with normal, sane people who hold a steady job and live in the

Left: an unexplained mist is captured on camera at Ravensworth Castle. Nothing was visible to the naked eye.

suburbs. What on earth is it that compels apparently ordinary people to spend their nights searching for signs of ghostly activity in frequently cold, draughty conditions? The weather rarely stops the determined investigator!

Ghost stories fascinate us. They appeal to our imagination and fears – we just love a good shiver. The majority of us have a tale to tell – an incident in our lives that we cannot explain. Paranormal or not, the appeal to both believers and sceptics is undeniable.

Investigating haunted properties, while sometimes nerve-wracking, as you will see, can help us face our own fears and sometimes go a little way towards answering questions that generally have no answers.

Did you see a ghost?

That question is a tough one, because there is no clear-cut definition of what a 'ghost' actually is! Most of us will conjure up a picture of something between Casper the Friendly Ghost and a bedsheet with eyeholes cut out. The image of the 'bedsheet' ghost is likely to date back to a time when those who couldn't afford coffins were lowered into their graves in shrouds. If the dead walked, as many believed, they would walk in their death-shroud.

Just as Coca Cola created the familiar image of Santa Claus, Hollywood and television started to change our perception of ghosts and spectres, mostly concentrating on the 'demonic', with possessions, murderous spirits and things that definitely do more than go bump in the night.

So what is it that paranormal investigators look for, and why do most of us cringe at the term 'ghost hunters' or more commonly 'ghost busters'?

In case you were wondering …

There are certain terms used within this book that may be confusing to the non-investigator.

Anomaly: something differing from the normal state of things.

Baseline test: A survey (such as temperature, EMF, etc) carried out before an investigation, as a control.

EMF: Electro-magnetic Flux

EVP: Electronic Voice Phenomena

Lock-off: a situation where a camcorder is attached to a tripod and left in an undisturbed location where the entrance is locked to prevent access.

Medium: a person claiming to be able to communicate directly with the dead.

Mist: anomalous mists are those that cannot be explained through natural occurrences or environmental factors (such as fog etc).

Night Vision: equipment configured to see in the dark, usually using infra red light.

Orb: a small ball of light usually not seen with the naked eye and often associated with areas of supernatural activity.

Picking Up: Information gained through mediumship or dowsing.

Provoke: (bait) when an investigator tries to verbally antagonise a suspected spirit to instigate activity. Not recommended unless said investigator is carrying a spare pair of underpants!

Vigil: a timed recorded investigative session.

Like other proto-scientific disciplines, paranormal investigation requires a serious mind, detailed research and careful recording of results. In reality, watching a full blown apparition walk down a corridor is somewhat unlikely … what the investigator is looking for are subtle environmental anomalies or changes that cannot be explained through rational means. These might include temperature fluctuations, moving lights or mists caught on camera or even, if the investigator is very lucky, the movement of an object. Studying these anomalies requires the right equipment, a talent for observation and above all patience; after all, these 'ghosts' don't jump through hoops and appear just because we ask them to!

Paranormal Investigation Equipment

What equipment does the average investigator have access to? Naturally this varies, from full CCTV and audio recording systems to just a pen, pad of paper and a nose for trouble. The following common tools are used by the Otherworld North East team:

The very basics

No investigator should be without a notepad, pen, clock or watch, a torch and a healthy supply of batteries. The most useful tools for investigating the paranormal are the human senses, and everything the investigator experiences should be recorded in as much detail as possible, including the precise timing of an event. As many investigations take place at night or in low light, torches are a necessity, and spare batteries should always be carried as they have a habit of draining completely at the precise moment you really don't want them to. At least one person in the group should be carrying a mobile phone and a first aid kit, in case the group runs into trouble (for example if someone trips and breaks an ankle).

Electro-Magnetic Flux (EMF) Meters

It is thought that the energy radiated by a 'ghost' will produce an anomaly in the environment's electromagnetic reading, so EMF meters are used. Of course, the environment has many naturally occurring EMFs. Electronic equipment that is switched on also produces EMFs so the meter is relatively useless unless used in conjunction with other detection equipment. Remember, an EMF meter is not a ghost detector, rather an environmental anomaly detector.

Carrying out an electro-magnetic survey at Ravensworth.

Ultrasound Meters

Based on the simple premise that animals such as cats and dogs seem to see and hear things that we certainly don't, these meters are designed to detect ultrasonics. Not yet a common tool in most investigation groups, they can provide interesting results. Just remember to check for bats!

Electronic Voice Phenomenon (EVP) Recorders and Audio Enhancers

Becoming increasingly popular as a detection tool, EVP recorders range from standard tape decks to highly sophisticated digital voice recorders. The premise is simple: set your dictaphone recording, and see what you get at the end! They are sometimes used in 'lock-off' situations (where a room is sealed off with equipment set inside to remove the possibility of human interference), or even to help record events during vigils. Some advanced Electro-magnetic Flux meters also have a built-in audio EVP capability, though they lack the recording capability, as do standard audio enhancers that are designed to augment the user's own hearing to high and low frequency sounds.

Thermometers

Two types of thermometer are useful during paranormal investigations: ambient air and non-contact spot thermometers. Ambient air thermometers measure the current air temperature in the area where they are situated; a non-contact thermometer measures the temperature of a specific spot (such as a person). To date temperature readings have provided the most common evidence of environmental changes in an area and the people within that area during alleged paranormal activity, with temperatures fluctuating wildly in sometimes sealed or controlled conditions. The theory behind this is pure physics: energy types, when altering states, sometimes draw heat from the air in order to facilitate the change, and at the same time can also release it as 'waste'. Obviously this is a very simplistic definition of a complicated process, but if we are to regard a 'ghost' as a form of energy then perhaps this theory goes a long way to explaining the most common of phenomena.

Trigger Objects

Perhaps the easiest of experiments to set up, trigger objects tend to be simple household items that are placed on a sheet of paper, carefully drawn around, and left in place to see if, at the end of an allotted period of time, they have moved. Such objects often include coins, keys, talc, dice and stacked sugar cubes – or 'emotive' objects such as children's toys or crucifixes, depending on the location and alleged activity. This is an experiment that works well as part of a lock-off.

Motion Detectors

These are devices that alert the group to movement in a given area, usually by the means of an infra-red 'tripwire' or other similar technique. They can be set to monitor whole rooms, or confined spaces such as doorways depending on the type of detector. Not recommended if investigating a residential property, as the detector alarm tends to be very loud … and always make sure you remember to pick them up at the end of an investigation, or the property owner won't be too pleased when he or she accidentally trips over them!

Cameras

A variety of cameras are often used on investigations. Digital cameras seem to pick up many 'phenomena' that normal 35mm cameras do not, specifically 'orbs' and other light anomalies. Many anomalies can be written off due to the way a digital camera is built and works, with examples such as lens flare, reflections off dust and moisture and in many

cases insects (though when zoomed you can often see the wings on the latter). Many argue that digital cameras shouldn't be used for this reason, but of course others claim that technology is finally advanced enough to capture elements of the supernatural. There is evidence to support both arguments, so perhaps digital photography is simply another tool that should be regarded with caution.

Standard 35mm photography has its own plus and minus points. On the plus side, the photographs taken are often much clearer and sharper, and of course you have the negatives to check against. On the minus side, it is also easy to create double exposures or 'movement anomalies' accidentally when using a long exposure often required in low light conditions. Double or long exposure also explains many of the 'ghosts' on old photographs, as simple movement can create a blurred, transparent effect, as can be seen in the example.

Camcorders

Camcorders are by far the most popular tool of the modern investigator. Equipped with night-vision capabilities he or she can record the investigation for playback and corroboration at a later date. Quality differs between camcorders, and again some can create interesting 'artefacts' that aren't on the original. However, from my standpoint, video evidence collected by the team during these investigations was excellent, and experts have been hard-pressed to refute the recorded findings.

Ghost pig? Or a classic example of double exposure in this photograph of Benwell piggeries.

Filming with a night-vision camcorder.

Dowsing Rods and Pendulums

Most groups use dowsing rods or pendulums, and both seem to obey basic rules of physics. Rod-dowsers for example have been employed by water companies, and some archaeologists use rods to try and detect walls buried and other artefacts. These rods seem to react to simple magnetic changes in the air and earth – and so paranormal investigators often use them in their search for spirit contact, working along the lines that if an 'anomaly' is present it will be manipulating and changing the same environmental factors.

Pendulums on the other hand are ancient tools of divina-tion or fortune telling. Normally a string or chain with a weighted balanced 'point', pendulums were used in Ancient Greece for detecting the gender of an unborn baby – and in more modern times were used for centuries to detect the gender of newborn rabbits in Northumberland.

Both rods and pendulums work on the same idea: they will swing one way to answer a question 'yes' and another for 'no'. Naturally this gives rise to accusations that the person holding the rods or pendulum is manipulating the tool: so careful observation (and filming) of a dowser should always take place.

The dowsers for the Otherworld North East team use the 'stop' command, working on the assumption that if the rods are swinging wildly or the pendulum swinging back and forth and the dowser commands 'stop', then it would take a large amount of energy to stop the tool dead in its tracks, especially when it is obviously not being manipulated by the dowser.

It is standard practice to monitor the dowser and his or her close environment with other tools, such as thermometers and electromagnetic meters. In theory, if a dowser is picking up activity, there should be a noticeable change in elements such as the temperature.

Mediums

A medium claims to have the ability to communicate with spirits, essentially acting as an 'intermediary' between the living and the dead. This ability may take the form of sight, hearing, smell or a combination of all the senses, from hearing a voice to seeing a full blown spirit, or just sensing a presence. The use of a medium is controversial, but often popular for its immediacy and drama.

The debate revolves around the difficulty of verifying the data being received. More importantly, the source of the information is called into dispute. This is especially true with more famous hauntings where information is in the public domain whether in books or on the internet, so if a medium 'picks up on' a name during an investigation, it is possible that he or she read the name somewhere beforehand, and the passing on of the information is either subconscious or in some cases, unfortunately, deliberate.

There is no denying that on at least a couple of Otherworld North East investigations a medium has revealed information,which he could not have known previously. He gave enough detail to make people who actually knew the facts very nervous indeed! In all these cases there were physical and environmental anomalies taking place, from temperature fluctuations to unexplained light anomalies on camcorder and photograph.

In essence, a medium is another resource, albeit one that walks, talks and thinks for itself. It can be frustrating for the team and the medium when they are picking up on activity that can not be verified by either the equipment to hand or historical research, and because of this many groups do not use one. The presence of a medium may add a certain psychological boost to an investigation, but the team should always remember that a medium is human, with human failings. Other equipment should not be ignored because it might seem less exciting!

Instinct

All of us have, deep within us, the basic survival instinct that our hunter-gatherer ancestors had – a most useful tool when

The investigation team enter a dark passage beneath Beamish Hall in the early hours of the morning, their imaginations firmly in check …

investigating the paranormal. Instinct is one of our most often ignored natural skills. It can detect changes in our environment, especially in the dark. Sounds, scents and movement not evident under normal circumstances become apparent, as these primitive instincts come to our aid.

Instinct can also prove problematic, especially for people who are scared of the dark or a little jumpy. Imagination has to be kept on a tight rein, as it is an easy step from 'sensing' something to believing it is there, especially in old, dark buildings where the shadows seem to come alive.

So, was it a ghost?

There is also the question of belief. Is a believer a more effective paranormal investigator than a sceptic? The believer's perceptions are wide open and they're more likely to experience subtle events, often missed by others. The downside is that many events that believers attribute to the paranormal can be explained in a perfectly rational manner. On the other side of the coin, the sceptic often misses events that cannot be explained, and valiantly tries to find explanations where none can be found. It has also been suggested by some researchers that having a true unbeliever in the team can decrease the team's chances of experiencing something. Of course unbelievers will respond that this proves that most perceived paranormal activity is merely suggestion! The role of the sceptic or unbeliever in a team can be a tough one, but it brings with it clarity of thought and the ability to say, 'no, it's only the wind closing the door!'

A warning

It is not the intention of this book to encourage people to try paranormal investigation for themselves as it may be sometimes dangerous physically (health and safety) and psychologically (suggestion is a powerful thing!). There are many groups countrywide offering members of the public the chance to join in investigations. Investigating with an established group is the best way to learn techniques and safe use of the equipment (for example, misuse of the temperature guns with laser sights can result in blindness or retina damage). If people do insist on undertaking their own investigations, it is imperative to go adequately prepared with full knowledge and permission from the owner of the property in question. Always tell someone where you are.

On location

Why were the venues in this book chosen for investigation? They represent a cross-section of allegedly haunted properties, from pubs to castles, chapels and hotels – across the whole of the North East; Northumberland, Tyne and Wear, County Durham and Teesside. Some are well known and obvious choices; others are previously unknown properties in the field of paranormal research and give a more balanced and often unexpected glimpse into the supernatural.

So please, turn on all the lights in the house and enjoy the collected ghost tales and paranormal case studies in Otherworld North East … and remember, next time you glimpse something moving behind you in the mirror, you may well not be alone!

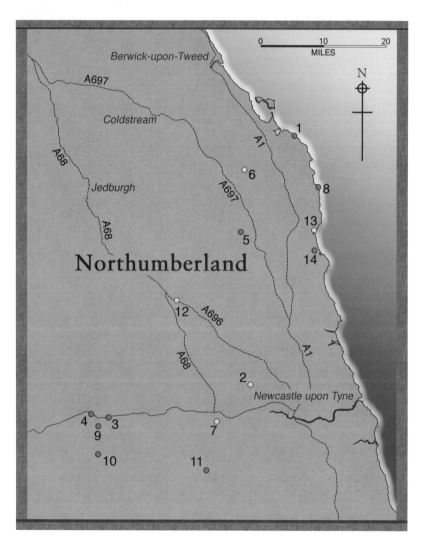

1. Bamburgh Castle

2. Case Study: The Bay Horse, Stamfordham

3. Bellister Castle

4. Blenkinsopp Castle

5. Callaly Castle

6. Case Study: Chillingham Castle

7. Case Study: Dilston Castle, Bridge and Chapel

8. Dunstanburgh Castle, near Craster

9. Featherstone Castle

10. Knaresdale Hall

11. Lord Crewe Arms, Blanchland

12. Case Study: Otterburn Tower Country House

13. Case Study: The Schooner Hotel, Alnmouth

14. Warkworth

1. Fortress of the Eastern Coast

Bamburgh Castle

Bamburgh Castle is one of the best-known castles on the Northumberland coast. Its impressive walls have been used in a number of television and film productions and its stunning location and size dominate the landscape. It is currently owned and occupied by the Armstrong family, who are allowing archaeological excavations of areas of the castle and the surrounding dunes. Legends associated with the castle concern a dragon, or rather a worm or wyrm, once said to plague the surrounding areas. There are also several ghost stories associated with the grounds, the best-known being that of the Green Lady, a slight female figure swathed in a green cloak who has been seen on a number of occasions tumbling down the old steps, clutching a bundle in her arms. People witnessing this have rushed to help her and her baby, but found nothing when they arrived at the spot. A Pink Lady is also said to haunt the grounds, legend claiming that she was the beautiful daughter of a Northumbrian King. Dressed in her finest pink gown, she threw herself from the highest tower when she found out that the man she loved had married another.

In the keep itself, the ghost of a fully armoured and armed medieval knight has been seen clanking through the darkened halls, perhaps simply going about duties that should have ended centuries ago. Other reported ghosts include an 18th century English soldier, a piano that plays itself and the shade of the castle's 18th century restorer John Sharp.

17

2. CLEANING UP

Case Study 23 April 2004
The Bay Horse, Stamfordham

The sleepy and scenic village of Stamfordham lies between Hexham and Newcastle upon Tyne, and traces its history back as far as 1220 with the first recorded reference to a church in the village. Archaeologists have identified Saxon (pre-1066) stonework in St Mary's church. The Northumbrian Swinburne family bought lands in the township in 1399. Stamfordham, like most villages and towns in the county, endured many years of raiding, war and bloodshed because of Scottish invaders, border reivers and associations with the Jacobite cause.

Stamfordham has a very strong link with Presbyterianism, building its own meeting house in 1742. The village had no Catholic church and it is said that the houses running along the northern side of the Stamfordham main street all have connecting doors, to allow escaping priests the best chance of survival in the days when Roman Catholicism was forbidden.

The Bay Horse Inn was built before 1590 as a fortified

The Bay Horse, Stamfordham.

farmhouse. Around the turn of the 17th century the farm was turned into a coaching inn. Nowadays en-suite bedrooms replace the Long Hall, and the lounge is where the original farm structure would have been. The area where the pool table stands is a more recent addition. As with many defensible structures, legends of secret tunnels beneath the inn have grown over the centuries.

It's a friendly pub, with more than one or two ghostly tales. These are what brought the Otherworld North East team to Stamfordham on 23 April 2004 – a nice warm night on which to spend the wee hours wandering the floors of the inn!

The owners described full apparitions crossing the restaurant area witnessed by more than one person; several people had seen things being moved in

The village of Stamfordham around 1910.

the kitchen, and disembodied footsteps had been heard on the main staircase. The landlord had caught strange lights on the CCTV security system, and several members of staff felt very uncomfortable when working in one of the rooms.

The team's guest medium immediately picked up on the presence of a priest in the pool area, and during a short walkaround described old staircases and figures rushing upstairs to old battlements, most of which the owner was able to verify. The tunnels were mentioned, and rod dowsing indicated a geological anomaly under the inn – where the

owner thought that the tunnel, if it existed, probably was.

The investigation started after closing time and was restricted largely to the ground floor, including kitchens, restaurant and bar. Rooms 2 and 6 on the first floor were also available; the others were in use by guests. The group split into two teams until the investigation ended around 5am.

Because the medium had picked up on a priest in the pool table area, we were hopeful of some results there despite it being the newest part of the building. All was quiet to start with, without temperature or EMF fluctuations, or anything showing on camera or camcorder. The group picked up EMF readings from the bar, easily identified as coming from the electric pumps, but a few team members reported a feeling of being watched. One of the camcorders began to go out of focus towards the kitchen, so the investigators moved there, halting briefly at the door when they heard a loud noise and turning in time to catch an impressive light anomaly crossing the restaurant area at speed (see film strip on page 21)! Further examination of the footage shows no visible 'wings' on the anomaly (which could indicate an insect), and no rational explanation of the light could be found.

Half an hour later, one of the investigators heard a strange knock coming from the back restaurant. Someone else asked anything present to give a sign. Yet another light anomaly flashed by (caught on nightvision camcorder), so we continued to ask (politely of course) for further signs ... whereupon there was a loud scraping in the adjoining bar sounding like a heavy bottle or glass being dragged across the bar or a table. A hasty investigation showed nothing untoward in the bar, but a there was a very strange feeling and a noticeable temperature drop, making us feel more than a little uncomfortable. Another crash was heard, this time from the kitchen, and as two of us headed towards the kitchen an 'orb' trailed its way across the screen of the camcorder right on cue.

Pendulum dowsing indicated there were two spirits present, neither of which was in any mood to 'chat' with the intrusive investigators. One of the group thought that the stronger spirit 'felt' like an old cook or servant, who was very territorial about the kitchen and the bar area.

During further investigation of the bar, one of the old wooden chairs by the window creaked loudly, and one of the

The bar area and the pool table. The team prepare for the investigation.

lights over the bar flashed on and off. This was accompanied by strange cracking noises from the area of the ladies' toilet, heard by one of the investigators and picked up on camcorder.

Many of the team felt uncomfortable and claustrophobic in the kitchens, perhaps because of the heat and the high electromagnetic field produced by the kitchen appliances. However, the strange sounds of shuffling footsteps, cameras refusing to focus and temperature fluctuations in the door area ranging from 12.5°-16.5°C all added to the feeling of a presence who wasn't overly pleased with strangers in her kitchen.

At the rear of the inn lies a back restaurant area, possibly where the old cellars used to be. EMF surveys produced a couple of anomalies which the team decided were caused by power cabling, though one investigator saw a peculiar flash of light which couldn't be explained. By 4am dowsing results were good; it was as if a spirit was playing with the pendulum, producing an erratic almost magnetised effect. At that point, low level temperature fluctuations were also recorded.

Upstairs, Room 2 was left as a lock-off area, but no anomalies were recorded.

Room 6 was another matter entirely. Furthest away from the rooms containing guests, both teams got some interesting results here. The EMF and photo survey showed nothing, so we tried pendulum dowsing. The dowser experienced small 22-25.5°C skin temperature fluctuations. The dowser connected with some unhappy spirits that objected to the team, although they did drop the temperature when requested to do so. Three distinct light anomalies were picked up on night-vision camcorder, and one of the investigators heard the sound of breathing behind him. In the early hours of the morning, Room 6 was also locked off with a night-vision camera and although the lock-off produced no new light anomalies it did pick up a number of cracking sounds, including a very loud and distinct noise which, on later inves-

tigation, seems disappointingly to be just the tape recorder switching itself off!

The Bay Horse investigation was an interesting night with both sound and light anomalies recorded. Close examination of the light anomalies caught on night-vision camera showed nothing that could be interpreted as dust or insects, and there are certainly no wings present! The light flashing over the bar when a sign was asked for is especially interesting as it didn't happen at any other time during the investigation.

The dowsing results were erratic but in some cases very strong. Unfortunately, not enough data was collected from the process to allow proper historical investigation but it did seem to indicate that the first floor of the inn at least, specifically Room 6, contained multiple entities.

One of the strongest indications of a presence on the ground floor is the light anomaly caught outside the kitchens, on film, the team clearly reacting to something behind them. And then there is the inexplicable sound of a glass or bottle being drawn across the bar.

Five still shots from the night vision video recorded outside the kitchen door looking into the restaurant. Carefully examine these frames and you should be able to see a bright light anomaly moving from right to left.

3. A Minstrel's End

Bellister Castle, Northumberland

The last recorded sighting of the Grey Man of Bellister Castle was over 150 years ago, but before that time the castle grounds and the forests around were known to be well and truly haunted by the ghost, whose appearance, it is said, foretold death. The origins of this spectre are shrouded in folklore, but it seems that during the reign of Elizabeth I, an old minstrel came to the Castle looking for shelter and food, for which he was willing to pay in song and story. However, the young Baron of Bellister drank too much, and his wine-fuddled mind began to play tricks on him, rousing paranoia and suspicions that perhaps the old man was an agent of his enemies, come to spy on him.

Perhaps the minstrel suspected the baron's intentions, or perhaps he noted the mood change, but after the castle settled down to sleep, he decided he'd chance his luck in the storm and headed out into the forest to find shelter. However, still fuelled by alcohol and suspicion, the Baron sent for him, only to find that he had fled. More convinced than ever that his guest had been a spy, the Baron let loose his hunting dogs. They caught up with the old minstrel where he sheltered in the forest, and so the tale goes, ripped him apart.

The Baron lived to regret his deed when the ghost of the minstrel became his shadow, following him wherever he went, looming over him with a stench of death, his wounds livid on his ghostly skin. The strain of being constantly stalked by his victim finally became too much for the Baron, and he died an early death.

The castle changed hands and a new family moved in, but the Grey Man could find no peace and continued to prowl the castle and the surrounding lands for generations, appearing to travellers and locals with hideously contorted features and a wail on his spectral lips. Perhaps he's still there.

Bellister Castle on a gloomy day around 1930.

4. A Buried Treasure

Blenkinsopp Castle, Northumberland

Blenkinsopp Castle's glory days were at the end of the 14th century; 200 years later the castle had become a mass of ruined walls and overgrown chambers. Over the years there were many attempts to restore the fortress, but all ended in failure and the only long term resident is its ghost.

There are many versions of the story of the White Lady but the most popular involves a young knight, Bryan de Blenkinsopp, whose only weakness was his love of wealth and his oath that he would never marry unless it was to a woman with a chest of gold heavier than ten of his strongest men could carry. Sir Bryan took his desire for gold and jewels to the Crusades, and years later returned home with an olive-skinned bride, and a massive chest of gold that was her dowry. The couple were happy at Blenkinsopp to begin with, until the young bride began to suspect that Sir Bryan had married her only for her father's gold. In revenge she hid the dowry chest deep within the castle – an act she lived to regret.

Infuriated, Sir Bryan made another vow – to leave and never return. He headed back to the Crusades, leaving his young wife behind, alone and suffering terrible grief and remorse, regretting her decision to hide her dowry. She waited years for her husband, but when news of his death reached her, she left Blenkinsopp, returning to her homeland.

Since then the White Lady of Blenkinsopp has haunted the castle grounds, searching for her husband, and attempting to reveal the location of the hidden dowry.

By the 1820s the fate of the Lady of Blenkinsopp Castle was little more than a fairy tale told around the fire in cold winter months. However, it seems that in the early 19th century, a herdsman and his family braved the legends of the ghost and set up a rough home in a couple of the less decayed rooms of the ruined castle.

The story goes that one night the parents were fast asleep, only to be awoken by a scream of terror from their son in the adjoining room. Mother and father rushed in to find him awake and shaking with fear, babbling about 'the white lady.' He told them that a well dressed lady in white had appeared and sat on his bed, kissed him and asked him to go with her – and if he did he'd be a rich man. The lady had buried a casket of gold in the vaults beneath the castle long ago, and could not find peace as long as it remained undiscovered. The boy's cry of terror as she reached for him had woken his parents – and scared the White Lady away.

There were no more reported appearances of the White Lady for 50 years or so until an unnamed woman visited the

Blenkinsopp Castle, Northumberland, from an early print.

inn at Greenhead, looking for permission to enter the ruins of the castle, as she'd had a dream of a lady in white telling her about a hidden treasure in the vaults. However, as the landowner was away at the time, she never got her permission, and left without exploring the ruins.

In the early 1970s it was reported that a tunnel had been found leading to underground vaults deep beneath the ruins. A workman checking its stability had barely been able to escape with his life when he was nearly overcome by gases that had been collecting there over the centuries. This seems to corroborate Margaret Tynedale's account in 1932 that 'some years ago' the vaults under the main tower were being cleaned out and a small tunnel was found. In that case the workman who ventured in was wise enough to get out quickly when the 'bad vapours put his light out.' The result was that the tunnel was sealed, possibly concealing forever the Blenkinsopp Treasure.

In the early 1800s Blenkinsopp Hall was built on a hill a mile north of the castle, on the site of a medieval tower. The Hall is said to be haunted by the apparition of a black dog, which heralds a death in the family of anyone who sees it.

Blenkinsopp Hall around 1930.

The ruins of Blenkinsopp Hall around 1980.

5. THE WICKED PRIEST

Callaly Castle, near Alnwick

Callaly Castle is a large private country house, with walls seven feet thick, carefully built around a 14th century Pele Tower. The structure we see today is mostly a 17th century skin. Above the central doorway is the coat of arms of the Clavering family who owned it from the middle ages until 1877. The reconstruction work was started by John Clavering in 1619 and finished by Trollope in 1676. The country house was continually altered until the late 19th century, and since then the only changes have been to make the rooms into apartments.

Of course, many ghostly tales have grown up around Callaly; the first seems to be about its original construction during which a disembodied voice told the workers to build elsewhere. Soon afterwards the walls collapsed. This continued until eventually they decided to build the castle on its current location. The most famous of its ghosts is known as the wicked priest, best described by Fleetwood:

Then there is Callaly Castle, the older part of which was the pele-tower of the Claverings. In this older part there was a walled-up room, near the roof; quite recently, so it's said, the wife of the gentleman now living there, to gratify her curiosity, had the wall of this room broken down, when the room was found to be quite empty; but the doing this, so it's said, set free a spirit, called the 'wicked priest' which has ever since annoyed the family with noises. These noises are sometimes so loud 'that you would think the house was being blown down,' and there are tramplings in the passages and noises in some of the bedrooms. It is also reported that the ghost, in the shape of a 'priest with a shovel hat,' has been seen.

Callaly around 1890 when it was owned by the Browne family. It is now converted into flats … and possibly also accommodates a 'wicked priest'.

6. The Most Haunted Castle in Britain

Case Study 25th-26th April 2004
Chillingham Castle, near Alnwick

Chillingham Castle near Alnwick in Northumberland is one of the most famous of all the northern castles, chiefly these days because of the 'paranormal activity' reported in the press.

The castle is associated with the Grey family and, like so many others, is bathed in the blood of Englishmen and Scots. In 1246 the Greys stormed and took the single-towered castle on the site. From then it proved an excellent staging post in the constant warring against the Scots, playing host to Kings and armies including Edward I in his campaign against William Wallace.

The tower wasn't converted into a proper fortress until 1344 when the castle received a Royal Licence to fortify the structure. It took four years of work but the result was a heavily walled castle capable of withstanding many an attack. The family gained the Earldom of Tankerville in 1409 when Ralph Grey helped capture the castle of Tanquaville on the mouth of the Seine. Only 11 years later Sir Thomas Grey, then commanding the armies of Bamburgh and Alnwick, declared independence for North East England; the royal answer from London was the siege of the castles by King Henry IV.

In 1513, the Greys lost other castles such as Heton and Wark to the Scots. They retreated back to Chillingham then joined the English troops who won victory against the Scots at Flodden Field. Twenty-three years later Chillingham once again came under siege, this time from a rebel army led by the Percys of Alnwick. The rebellion was put down, but not before Chillingham suffered heavy damage from cannon-fire.

Members of the Grey family were killed in the service of King Charles II. However, Charles ordered the execution of the Earl's elder brother – understandably because Grey had

Chillingham Castle and its courtyard, from a 19th century print.

signed Charles' death warrant! Another Lord of Chillingham plotted against James II, but despite being condemned to death in the Tower of London, he survived to become the First Lord of the Treasury.

Chillingham became a barracks during the Second World War and then fell into neglect until it came into the hands of its present owner, Sir Humphrey Wakefield Bt, who has spent the last 20 years painstakingly restoring and regenerating the estate.

Lady Leonora Tankerville, writing in 1925, gives us our first real glimpse into hauntings at Chillingham Castle. In her *Ghosts of Chillingham Castle* she describes skeletons found in wall recesses and preserved bodies, that disintegrated upon coming into contact with the air, discovered in walled-up dungeons. Lady Tankerville also described the Radiant Boy, perhaps Chillingham's most famous ghost. She says that at midnight, anyone in the Pink Room would see a young boy dressed in blue and surrounded by light, and hear his screams of pain echoing around the castle. The bones of a boy had been found in a wall in that room, and once they had been re-interred in consecrated ground, the Radiant Boy was never seen again.

Lady Mary Berkeley, from the time of Charles II, is said to roam the halls and corridors of Chillingham looking for her husband, Ford, who had run away with her sister Henrietta. Ford's departure with his mistress caused a great scandal and a lawsuit, and the result is that Mary's spectre still haunts the castle, often accompanied by the rustle of her

dress and a blast of cold air.

Lady Tankerville also reports that a White Lady haunted the 'inner pantry', her pale spirit asking constantly for a glass of water, and that there were many places in the castle with a heavy oppressive atmosphere and a feeling of doom. One such place was one of the maids' rooms, in which a cook had committed suicide. Beneath that room was the library, where voices had been heard muttering and arguing when no-one was present.

But what evidence do we have for the Chillingham hauntings? The castle has been subject to much scrutiny over recent years, including investigation by the Society of Psychical Research which looked into the case of the Radiant Boy's supposed burial in the local church. Sadly they could find no record of any bones being buried there in the decades around the date suggested for the finding of the remains. However, in looking into the phenomena in the castle, Ken Smith, investigator for the Society spoke to Mr Cyril Robson, a guide at Chillingham, in November 2000.

Ken reports: 'I asked Mr Robson if he had ever experienced any phenomena at the castle himself, as he had at that time been a guide at the building for 11 years. He told me that on multiple occasions he had heard unaccountable footsteps, which were distinct and in his opinion definitely female, coming from different parts of the building. They were accompanied by what seemed to be the rustling of a dress or skirt, and that he would bet, a "pound to a penny" that the material making the sound was taffeta or a similar fabric. Before his retirement he had been a draper and he was familiar with the sound of clothing materials. The swish which accompanied the footsteps was like a "rising and falling sound".'

The footsteps had been heard by Mr. Robson over a dozen times, always when he knew he was alone, and from all areas of the castle except the western side where the converted apartments are. On one occasion the guide had actually found himself jingling the coins in his pocket in time to the footsteps, and noted that the swish of taffeta was at its loudest between steps, drawing the conclusion that the two were definitely linked. He also said that he was sure the shoes worn by the 'spirit' were leather, going as far as to say it sounded like old fashioned leather, rather than the 'ring' of modern shoes.

Ken goes on: 'Another phenomenon he had experienced were mysterious voices coming from the direction of the former chapel (now the library), which was beside the Great Hall. The voices seemed to be having a conversation but no words were discerned. He had heard this unaccountable talking on multiple occasions: "You cannot hear words," said Mr Robson, "only a mumble". The longest of these mumbled conversations – male voices that seemed to be having a heated discussion – lasted about 18 seconds, though on average they lasted little more than ten, and usually once he concentrated on the voices they faded away.'

On several occasions, Cyril Robson also experienced what felt like someone standing behind him, easily within touching distance, but of course no-one was there.

According to Ken, 'Mr Robson (who was then aged 73) maintained he had never felt nervous in the castle. He had "never felt any qualms". He did not appear to have been frightened by his experiences. I found Mr Robson to be an impressive witness, and some of the details about the alleged phenomena which he gave to me were not contained in Leonora Tankerville's booklet *The Ghosts of Chillingham*. It must be remembered that when I spoke to him he had been a guide at the castle for 11 years during the summer months and was therefore familiar with the place and in my view not likely to be nervous or unduly imaginative about the stories or the building itself.'

The two-night investigation on 25 and 26 April 2003 into the paranormal events at Chillingham Castle was run by UK Ghost Investigators. This was my very first investigation, and it proved eventful!

During the first night's investigation, the Chilling Dungeon, or alleged torture chamber was investigated thoroughly several times during the night. The first incident occurred at 9.30pm when the main door to the chamber opened and closed four times by itself, and a cold spot was found outside the door – cold enough for the breath of the team to start steaming.

Chillingham's 'chilling' dungeon with a multitude of torture implements.

The first experiment in the Chilling Dungeon was table-tipping, where team members sit around a small table (in this case a plastic picnic one!) and place their fingers lightly on the surface, while asking any spirit present to tip, hit or otherwise move the table. During this experiment, one of the team saw a shadowy figure watching them from the doorway for about ten seconds at the same time as another team mem-ber reported a touch to his elbow then a tugging at his leg. No-one else other than the team was present.

Later in the night, a dowser picked up the spirit of a man who had died as a result of torture, though not in the room itself (not surprisingly as this room was probably a dairy). UKGI's leader and medium also picked up on a man called John. An EVP recorder was set later in the night, and when the audio was reviewed it contained the sound of someone opening the door and walking around, though a quick check with security convinced the team that no-one had been in there.

The team's base room was the tea room; a very cold room, even with the open fire blazing away to ward off the chill. The team medium once again saw John, the spirit she'd seen in the Chilling Dungeon, pacing back and forth across the Minstrel's Gallery overlooking the room. One of the other team members also picked up on a female, Judith, sitting by the fireplace.

In the corridors leading to the apartments, various team members described the feeling of being watched, and one or two light anomalies were caught on digital camera, though the air was a little dusty. One of the investigators also saw a shadow detach itself from the group and head out of the door.

The dairy room seemed to accommodate a presence that made many team members emotional and breathless. Pendulum dowsing revealed the presence of a little boy named Arthur, who apparently had been killed in 1653 in that room by a dog, and relived his death every night on the stroke of midnight (curiously like the Radiant Boy legend). The team's medium reported being gently pushed out of the room by what felt like a child after picking up a dark presence around her … perhaps it was whatever was picked up in the adjoining Little Dungeon growling on the EVP recorder!

The team also had access to the Grey Rooms, allegedly the most haunted part of Chillingham. The medium picked up on a little boy called 'George' or 'Georgie', while the camcorder went out of focus nearly every time an investigator asked a question – a door also slammed loudly, and another EVP recording picked up the distinct voice of a woman saying 'Elizabeth Talbot'. Interestingly, historical research into the Grey family reveals that around 1379 the 24-year-old Elizabeth de Talbot married into the Grey family … a happy coincidence or an echo from the past caught on tape perhaps?

The following night's vigils started at 9pm after a briefing in the tea room where, new to all this paranormal investigations lark, I was a bit unnerved by the feeling of being watched from the Minstrel's Gallery.

The torture chamber was the first focus for the teams, but very little was found in there except a lot of yellow 'orbs' on digital camera, more than likely dusty residue from the straw covering the floor. Table-tipping was attempted again, but with no results and there was little feeling to the place, so one of the team leaders decided to lock the room off with an EVP recorder.

In the tea room the medium picked up a strong vindictive spirit, whom she identified as Mary Berkley (Chillingham's famous Grey Lady) and described her as 'the boss' of the castle. Two separate dowsing sessions took place using the same questions, but away from each other's line of sight or earshot, and both dowsers picked up on a Mary who disliked the team medium and threatened to follow her around. At the same time, the medium was drawing the woman she could see. The dress she drew was identified as being in a painting of Mary which was in a room she'd not yet been into. At the times the medium said the 'lady' was present at her shoulder I could certainly feel a cold spot precisely where she was supposedly standing.

In the corridors between the apartments an investigator once again saw a dark shadow move off towards the door, and the team dowsers contacted two spirits who had died from illness; a 29 year old woman who had perished in 1664 and a 30 year old male who had died in 1737. No names were forthcoming, so it is impossible to verify this information. EVP tests were also conducted in the corridors with no results.

At midnight, the group split into pairs and spread out through the castle to listen for the cries of the Radiant Boy, but by 12.10am nothing had been heard or caught on EVP so the investigators returned to their vigils.

The Dairy Room once again produced interesting, if conflicting, dowsing results, with a 35 year old maid named Laura saying that she had died in 1522 as a result of an accidental fall. Another dowser once again picked up on the 12-year-old Arthur, but this time identified his date of birth as 1629 and his year of death as 1641 – 1641

26/04/2003

The minstrel's gallery on the second night around 2am. Note the light anomalies (top) caught on digital camera. The fact that two of them are 'cut off' makes lens flare unlikely. I felt I was being watched as I took the photograph.

had been identified as his year of birth, not death, the night before. The dowsing indicated that Arthur enjoyed playing with visitors, that he could move things, and that the room marked the area where he used to play in life. During communication with Arthur, a loud metallic clang was heard in the corner of the room, but no source for this sound could be found.

The next room was my 'favourite' (for want of a more

appropriate word): the little dungeon. The room is tiny, and must have been little more than a holding cell, with a very small hole in the floor now covered by a steel grate. The hole leads to a dungeon, below which lies a pit with, according to legend, the bones of over a dozen prisoners still buried in its fill. Two of us sat in the little dungeon for some time, making an EVP recording while we asked questions. We were mildly concerned as no cameras would take photographs (they would jam or drain of power). The EVP results were interesting, especially when we put the recording mic for the EVP down through the grate. Though nothing was audible to the human ear, the sound recording seemed to contain a gabble of voices, not all of which were speaking English! During this episode the temperature also dropped rapidly, falling by 10°C in a matter of seconds.

We tried pendulum dowsing in the cell, picking up on a cold and hungry spirit who said that he had been falsely imprisoned there for allowing the horses to escape from the stables. This concerned me, especially when the dowser located the spirit leaning against one of the corners – as when I entered the room I thought I saw a figure huddled there for a brief second. The spirit's name was Fabian, he was French, and spelled his name 'Feb'. He apparently had died in the main dungeon in 1634, alongside the man who had committed the

The entrance to the real Chillingham holding cell.

'crime', whom he called Michael. Fabian claimed that there were 11 other spirits who haunted that area, which was why so many people felt uncomfortable in, or even drawn to the little dungeon and the room below.

Fabian was aware of the other spirits said to wander the grounds of Chillingham, and identified a 'Mary' as one of the strongest.

Interestingly, six months after the investigation, I took a friend who was a developing medium to visit the castle. She too identified the little dungeon as a centre of activity, and picked up on a man who dealt with the horses and who was French, not English. Though she couldn't get a name, could this have been independent corroboration of the dowsing results?

In early 2004, Living TV made their first *Famous and Frightened* TV show at Chillingham Castle; a three day 'reality TV' event where celebrities undertook tasks and were slowly voted out, the prizes being donations to charities. On the first night of the show, Living TV's medium purportedly contacted the Grey Lady and 'sent her to the light', in theory dispelling Chillingham's most famous ghost. However, if the tales that have continued to be told are true, (and certainly subsequent visits to the castle still reveal the same sense of her presence) someone forgot to tell the Grey Lady that she'd been exorcised …

A very strange anomaly is captured on digital camera in the tea rooms.

I was about to take a shot of the team when I was suddenly aware of movement above. This photograph was the result of a hasty turn about. The picture below is an enhancement of the object (and look … no wings!).

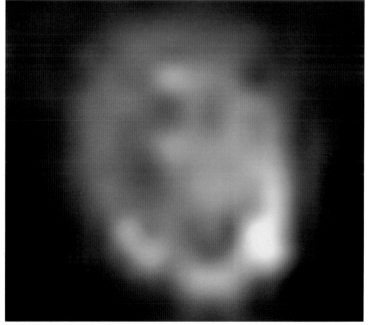

7. The Thundering Earl

Case Study June 18th 2004
Dilston Castle and Chapel, near Corbridge

The Hall is behind us, and its tragic story haunts the place. It is but a generation since the trampling of hoofs and the clatter of harness was heard on the brink of the steep here, revealing to that trembling listener that 'the Earl' yet galloped with spectral troops across the haugh. Undisturbed, as the reverent hands of his people had laid him and his severed head, the Earl himself had rested hardly in the little vault for a whole century; yet the troops have been seen by the country people over and over again as they swept and swerved through the dim mist of the hollow dene.

So wrote the Reverend Heslop in the *Monthly Chronicle*, 1888. In 1715, the Earl of Derwentwater rode from Dilston with his troops to take part in the Jacobite Rising. Almost 300 years later the ghosts of the Earl and his troops are still said to ride around the area, and the Earl and his young bride sometimes haunt a small bridge in the grounds.

The story of James Radcliffe is tragic. The young Earl was no lover of war, but was persuaded to ride into battle by his wife, who lived to regret her words when James failed to return home. Since then her anxious shade is said to move between the tallest towers of the castle and across to the chapel, keeping a lookout for him.

Over recent years, the grounds of Dilston Castle and Chapel, now part of the MENCAP college near Corbridge, have been the site of alleged paranormal activity, from a man wearing a long curled wig (as the Earl himself would have worn) seen staring out of one of the castle windows, to cold spots and strange feelings of being watched in the chapel. A couple of years ago, a small group of people camped by Dilston Bridge at Halloween in the hope of seeing one of the many spectres reported there, and claim to have seen a man shining in moonlight run across the bridge and quite literally through the temporary gate set up across its width. However, this was no ancient ghost, but described as a man in what looked like a jogging suit! There have also been reports of mysterious shadowy figures chasing people down

Dilston Castle and bridge.

the roads around the Hall and college – generally reports from reliable people with no wish or need to make anything up.

On 18 June 2004 the Otherworld North East investigation team arrived at the historic site and divided into three groups for vigils covering the restored chapel (with its underground crypt), the ruined castle and of course the grounds and the bridge.

At the castle the team noted some rather annoyed bats on the ground floor while they carried out the electromagnetic and temperature survey of the building. One of the team members, a sensitive, thought that she could sense an 'Ann' or 'Anna' in the close vicinity.

The group decided try pendulum dowsing and results confirmed there was indeed an Anna present. The instruments recorded one team member's body temperature fluctuating by 12.5°C, an unnatural change that should have seen her fall unconscious! After the dowsing the group set up trigger coins in the fireplace to see if they would move, and two investigators saw moving streaks of light through the doorway.

In the early hours of the morning, the group did more electromagnetic tests in the castle, this time combined with ultrasonics – the latter of course picking up the bats who were by this time getting rather irritated by all the flashing torches. One little fellow decided to relieve himself over one of the investigators (me), much to the amusement of the team!

Once settled, the investigators started pendulum dowsing, giving the visiting North Pennines Trust archaeologist the

The Earl's Bridge, Dilston, c.1900, the scene of many ghostly sightings.

first go in the castle's cell. The pendulum responded with extremely strong swings; the video footage shows that the dowser was not manipulating it or moving at all. Dowsing identified a Francis Radcliffe who wasn't at all happy that we were there: and at that point the ambient air temperature dropped by 3°C, sending a chill through the group. Francis said he was happy with the work that had been done to Dilston, and that he wasn't buried at Dilston (he's thought to lie in a church in nearby Corbridge). He also said he was happy the archaeologist was present, as he recognised him from his time excavating the castle!

We did dowsing in the room across from the cell – the one with all the bats. Again, the results were strong and identified an Edward, who claimed that six other spirits walked the Dilston grounds, and would periodically be seen. One final attempt was made at dowsing, this time by me. It was a strange sensation as it felt as if the chain I was holding was being tugged, almost as if the pendulum was being pulled in answer to my questions. The answers made little sense, as the dowsing identified a little boy who claimed to be a Radcliffe but not a Radcliffe, so I pretty much dismissed it. However, subsequent historical research by Mary-Rose Ridley has uncovered an obscure reference that indicates a bastard child was taken in by the Radcliffes in the same era that I mentioned in the dowsing. Does this explain a Radcliffe that was not a Radcliffe?

Time spent on the infamous bridge across the Devilswater also proved interesting, though the group certainly wasn't confronted by hordes of spectral horsemen! Instead, a couple of light anomalies were witnessed, including an odd green light in one tree, seen by two members of the team. Three investigators saw two very dark shadowy figures at the north end of the bridge who simply vanished. The area was quickly checked but no-one was in the vicinity. The electromagnetic sweep showed nothing out of the ordinary, and temperature gauges were useless because of the icy air on the bridge. Pendulum dowsing indicated the presence of James Radcliffe and his wife who simply wished to be left in peace … as well as a a young fellow who claimed to have died in 1663 on or near the bridge.

The vigils in the chapel were the most inactive parts of the night, despite the fact that in two spots in particular, the top of the steps leading down to the crypt and the altar area,

A view of Dilston Castle at dawn… perhaps a little early for moths to be out. This 35mm shot has captured an odd shape (bottom left). Could this have been an insect, or is it something else?

staff had reported cold spots and the feeling of being watched. Interestingly though, the only two light anomalies I caught on the night were in those precise spots!

There was really only one result: at 1.34am, one of the team picked up a woman by the name of Anna who claimed to have followed them from the castle; at the same time the dowser's skin temperature dropped from 22 to 15°C. The dowsing also revealed that one of the woman's children had been murdered by a man named John, who was buried in the crypts. Interestingly, there are two burials of unidentified people in the Dilston crypts. Could the mysterious John actually be buried in the crypt? Only time and a lucky break in historical research will reveal the answer.

Left, a view of the newly restored chapel. On the right, the interior of the chapel, looking towards a spot that the staff find uncomfortable. One of the only light anomalies caught on digital camera can be seen below the window. Careful examination by computer shows the anomalies to be solid and three-dimensional ... (without wings!).

8. ELEVEN STROKES

Dunstanburgh Castle, near Craster

The remnants of Dunstanburgh Castle are some of the most evocative ruins on the Northumberland Coast. It's a good mile walk from nearby Craster (famous for its kippers!) to the site of what was once the county's biggest castle. The castle was built in the early half of the 14th century, and saw a lot of military activity during the War of the Roses when it was besieged with cannon fire at least five times. What was left of the castle at the end of the war would have been too expensive to restore so it fell into a state of decay.

As is to be expected, the ruins are said to be haunted by at least three ghosts. The most famous is the Dunstanburgh Grey Lady who has been seen wandering around inside the castle grounds on numerous occasions, usually accompanied by a blast of chilling air (though how you can tell the difference with the blustery direct north sea winds, who knows!). This unfortunate soul is said to be Margaret of Anjou, wife of King Henry VI, a headstrong woman who bemoaned her imposed exile in Scotland.

Dunstanburgh's second ghost is said to be that of the castle's builder, Thomas Earl of Lancaster, who was executed for treason in 1322 on the orders of King Edward II whom he'd

Dunstanburgh Castle around 1728, from an old print.

managed to annoy. Thomas's spectre carries its head, which bears a look of intense agony and horror – perhaps not surprising because it took eleven strokes of the executioner's blade to part it from Thomas's shoulders.

The third ghost has his origins in myth rather than history. According to the story a young knight by the name of Sir Guy (known as the Seeker) took shelter in the castle during a storm. He was approached by a wizard, who told him that a beautiful young maiden needed to be rescued from the depths of the castle. The wizard led him into the Great Hall, and instructed him to choose between a sword and a horn. Whichever he chose would be the instrument of the maiden's release. Already armed with a keen-bladed sword, the knight picked the horn and blew it. At that point, the legend says, Sir Guy was confronted by 100 armed warriors in white, whereupon he dropped the horn in shock, and abruptly found himself outside the castle with no way back in. There are numerous versions of this story; sometimes it is King Arthur and his knights who are woken from their slumber by the horn, or a great treasure is bestowed on Sir Guy.

However each story ends the same way, with the forlorn knight continuing after death to search for his prize. Tales of his tormented shouts and cries are still said to be heard at the stroke of midnight.

9. RIDE OF THE BRIDAL PARTY

Featherstone Castle, near Haltwhistle

Featherstone Castle traces its origins back to the 13th century, though it was much added to in the 19th century, and given its romantic battlements and turrets. The grounds are reputed to be the haunt of an annual ghostly event: the ride of an ill-fated bridal party through buildings and walls as they follow the path they would have taken to their deaths in a nearby glen. The tale begins 'hundreds of years ago' when it is said a Baron of Featherstonehaugh set up an arranged marriage for his daughter Abigail. However, the young woman had already fallen deeply in love with another man, a certain Ridley of Hardriding (with whom the Baron was feuding), and in fear of his daughter doing something rash, the Baron made sure she was married immediately to the groom he had chosen for her. Following tradition, the bridal party set out to ride around the boundaries of the barony, their final destination being a great feast back at the Castle.

However, none of the bridal party set eyes on the castle again. Ridley of Hardriding lay in ambush with his retainers in a small glen called Pynkinscleugh, determined to win Abigail back by force, but the ambush went badly and all were killed, including Abigail who was accidentally struck down trying to stop the bloodshed. It is said that the blood of bride, groom and their slayer flowed down into a hollow stone, whereupon ravens drank from it – and was called from that day the Raven's Stone.

Meanwhile, the Baron and the staff of Featherstone Castle awaited the return of the party with growing concern, the banquet growing cold. Eventually, the servants retired to their beds leaving the Baron to await his daughter and her groom. He sat in his great chair at the end of the hall and began to drift off to sleep.

At the stroke of midnight, his fitful sleep was disturbed by the thundering of hooves. Relieved, he watched as the bridal party, led by Abigail, entered the hall. When all the guests were seated the Baron noticed that something wasn't quite right. Not a single word was spoken, or goblet raised. This made the Baron look more closely at his daughter and guests.

Horrified, he realised that he was looking at a hall of ghosts, and that his beloved daughter and all his guests were dead. Stunned, he crossed himself and suddenly a hurricane roared through Featherstone Castle. In the morning, the perplexed servants found the Baron curled up on the floor, his sanity quite gone. When the wind had subsided the Baron had found himself all alone in his hall.

The story goes that the bridal party forever retraces the route they took to Pynkinscleugh; the sound of ghostly hooves churning the mud and grass and pale apparitions being seen. However, though this tale is the most well known, made famous in *The Monthly Chronicle* of 1888, it is by no means the sole haunting.

It is said that Featherstone is also haunted by the groaning cries of the knight Sir Reginald Fitz Urse who died in the castle's Great Tower where he was left to starve to death, and also by the Green Lady, a spectre said to wander the corridors dressed in a sweeping green and brown gown.

10. THE KNARESDALE CURSE

Knaresdale Hall, Northumberland

Knaresdale Hall is a 17th century house four miles south of Haltwhistle in the South Tyne moors, the ancient seat of the Pratt family. The ghost tale of Knaresdale is typical of a classic haunting, with murder striking amidst stormy weather where thunder clashed and lightning lit the hall and surrounding forest.

The tale is undated, and begins with a pretty girl catching the eye of the lord of the manor. Despite her protests he gained her parents' consent to marry her. The newlyweds often argued and fought, but things took a turn for the better when the lord's niece and nephew came to stay at the hall. Or so it seemed. Unknown to the rest of the household, the young mistress of the hall and her husband's nephew had begun a passionate affair … until the niece caught them kissing. The girl, a sensible and loyal sister, decided not to tell anyone of her discovery, worried that the lad would be turned out of the hall (at the very least!) and instead kept the knowledge to herself, though she did try to bring her brother to his senses. Unfortunately for her, the two lovers had other plans – to kill her to protect their secret.

One night soon after this plan was made, a great storm hit the area, and the mistress of the house, hearing a door banging from one of the outbuildings, requested the lord of the manor to ask his niece to close it. Dutifully, the young girl, wrapped in a cloak, headed out into the storm to find the offending door, only to be waylaid by her brother and thrown into the pond by the hall, where he held her under until she drowned.

Knowing nothing of this, the lord fell asleep, only to be awoken in the middle of the night by the howl of one of his dogs, and there, by the kitchen fireplace was the spectre of his niece, wringing water out of her hair. As he approached to speak with her, she simply vanished.

Soon afterwards, it is said that Knaresdale Hall seemed cursed, with the murderous mistress of the house falling ill and slowly losing her sanity. In her ravings, she often mentioned the pond, so the hall staff dragged it and found the remains of the young niece.

However, it seems that merely finding her body and giving her a Christian burial was not enough to give the ghostly niece peace. It is said that on the anniversary of her death she can be seen by the pond and that the main door of the house can always be found open, even if it has previously been locked.

11. DARING DOROTHY

Lord Crewe Arms, Blanchland

The Lord Crewe Arms, in the picturesque Derwent Valley village of Blanchland, is one of the most well-documented of all haunted buildings in the North East. Its rich history can still be sensed in the atmosphere of the building. The earliest part of the Lord Crewe Arms is thought to be 12th century; it was part of the Abbey of Blanchland founded by Premonstratensian Monks (otherwise known as White Canons, Norbertines and Premonstrants, an order founded by St Norbert at Prémontré in France in 1119). The hotel is the former abbot's lodge, kitchens and guesthouse.

With the dissolution of the Abbey in 1536, the Northumbrian Radcliffe family bought the estates and buildings, passing them onto the Forsters of Bamburgh in 1623. At this point, the Abbey began to decay and the other buildings were converted into houses for the village. The building which is now the Lord Crewe Arms became a manor house, complete with priest hole in the huge fireplace. In 1701 tragedy struck the Forsters. The last direct male heir of the family was murdered in Newcastle and the

Blanchland Estate passed to his sister Dorothy, and his nephew Thomas.

Two years earlier, Dorothy had married Lord Crewe, Bishop of Durham, who, in 1704, bought both the Bamburgh and Blanchland estates from Dorothy and Thomas. Thomas was appointed Jacobite commander during the 1715 uprising, and surrendered at Preston. He was taken to London and imprisoned in Newgate Gaol, only to escape three days

The Lord Crewe Arms, Blanchland, photographed around 1900. Dorothy Forster's Tower is to the right.

before he was due to stand trial. He was helped by his sister, who, confusingly, was also called Dorothy.

In the current building, only the Crypt Bar and the rooms above date from the 12th century; the rest were built and developed in the 17th century by Lord Crewe. The ghost of Dorothy, daring sister of Thomas Forster, is said to return to her old rooms at night.

Legend has it that Thomas and his sister returned from Newgate Gaol and Thomas hid in the priest hole in the manor's chimney (now the Hilyard Room), until he escaped the country. He died in France without ever returning home again. His sister haunts the apartments where she used to live, awaiting the return of her brother from exile. Many visitors who have stayed in her old rooms (now the Bamburgh Room), have reported her pale and sad ghost imploring them to take a message to her brother, still in France, to say that he could return home again and that all is well.

Others have reported a white-robed monk kneeling in prayer in one of the rooms that belonged to the old Abbot's lodging area. Strange footsteps and lights have been seen in parts of the building known to be empty. In more recent months, a tourist having a quiet drink in the small bar off the Crypt Bar reported feeling the presence of a woman behind her, walking from the fireplace, towards the drinkers.

Above, the Lord Crewe Arms c.1907, and below, around 1900.

12. An Ancient Fortress

Case Study June 25th 2004
Otterburn Tower Hotel

Otterburn Tower Country House is a grand hotel in the Northumbrian town of Otterburn in the heart of Redesdale. The first building is said to have been built by a cousin of William the Conqueror in 1086. It is a magnificent building, set in 32 acres of land, fronted by terraced lawns, with 17 rooms including a master suite that was once the Tower's library.

Like many such buildings in Northumberland, Otterburn Tower was the focus of war and bloodshed for centuries. The original pele tower was built in 1308 by the Umfraville family; they were charged with the protection of Redesdale and nearby Tynedale against 'wolves and enemies'. In 1388 the tower survived its bloodiest attack from marauding Scots following the Battle of Otterburn; the battlefield itself just lies one mile north-west of the tower. The next few centuries saw the Tower amidst the constant Anglo-Scottish battle for Northumberland, but in the late 16th century the Hall family, a powerful Redesdale clan, acquired it.

The most famous of the Halls was Squire Mad Jack Hall, a Justice of the Peace who, in 1716, was hanged at Tyburn for his Jacobite sympathies, despite being reprieved five times and claiming that he was simply leaving a Justices' meeting when he was surrounded by the mustering Jacobites. However his sympathies towards the cause were well known. When he heard that the Jacobites were gathering he was in a meeting in Alnwick, and left so quickly that he left his hat behind. His initials are still carved above one of the original doors at the Tower.

Otterburn Tower c.1890.

During the 18th century, the fortress was rebuilt by Reginald Hall of Catcleugh into a more spacious country house, though it still incorporated the pele tower, the building work was done along the lines of a basic Scottish square farmhouse design. Archaeologists have said some of the earlier fortress can still be seen in the building's makeup.

Further extensions were carried out in the early 1900s when antiquarian Howard Pease bought the Tower, and constructed the lodge at the gates. In 1947 a Mr Halliday from Bellingham converted the Tower into a hotel, and it seems to have been about this time that the tales began.

For decades there have been stories concerning happenings in the Tower, ranging from strange noises and smells to uncomfortable feelings and the sensation of being watched. A traditional Grey Lady has been seen wandering the corridors, and once marching footsteps were heard in an area known at the time to be unoccupied.

So who haunts the corridors and rooms of the Otterburn Tower County House and Hotel? Could it be the spectre of Mad Jack Hall himself, or Sir Walter Scott the poet and songwriter, who visited the tower in 1812 while gathering inspiration for his poem *Rokeby*?

The hotel closed in 1996 and was bought by the present owner in August 1998. It was renovated and refurbished before re-opening in June 1999. Since that time there have been fewer tales of its ghostly occupants, so perhaps the changes have laid at least some of the building's ghosts to rest ... but by no means all.

On the night of Friday 25 June, 2004, the Otherworld North East team went to Otterburn Tower to discover if the hotel was still as paranormally active as the history books

Otterburn Tower Hotel on the evening of the investigation, 25 June, 2004.

indicated. Naturally, the team didn't have access to all the rooms – especially with a wedding planned for the next day.

The Otherworld team, accompanied by two members of the hotel staff, and a guest, split up to cover as much ground as possible during the night. One of the staff claimed to be a medium and proved an interesting addition to the team for the night! Especially exciting was the news that earlier that week, a shut and bolted window in the ground floor bar had blown open, and when the couple sitting beside it had turned to close it, their drinks had been swapped on the table in front of them! The woman on duty at the bar at the time confirmed that no one had been playing tricks on the surprised couple, and she couldn't work out why or how the window had opened in the first place.

The owner gave the team a tour of the building and the grounds before the vigils started. Certain areas such as the cellars were crossed off the investigation list because of too much 'interference' from the beer pumps and other electrical equipment. Soon after 11pm, when most of the guests had gone to bed, the investigation started.

Initially the bridal suite was classed as an off-limits area because the bride's dress was hanging up in there. However the bride asked three team members, including me, to hold a short vigil to put her mind at rest – she'd heard the room was the focus of ghostly activity in the hotel and she was due to spend the following night in there. A camcorder was set overlooking the room while EMF and temperature surveys were conducted, none of which found any anomalies. However, one of the bridal party told the team that she'd been sensing something in there all day, so it was decided to make an attempt at communication. The bride bravely asked anything present to show itself by either a light or sound, but with no

results. We tried pendulum dowsing, and though the response was very weak it indicated an adult female who was a chambermaid. Nevertheless, that vigil ended in a much happier bride!

Nearby, room 8 proved rather interesting. There were two separate vigils during the night and as usual the two teams did not share their experiences until the end of the investigation. The first vigil took place just before 3am, once again with no EMF results. The guest medium said she felt very uncomfortable approaching the door to the room, and was reluctant to enter. Once in there, one of the dowsers began getting strong results, and picked up a female who had died in 1830 at the age of 32, murdered by her husband in the grounds. Dowser and medium agreed on the name Eliza James, the medium announcing that Eliza been pushed down stairs, which broke her spine and killed her. Unfortunately no historical records have been found of such a woman, but the next group, ignorant of what had been found in the previous vigil, picked up on an adult female, who claimed to have been in contact with the earlier group, and indicated that she had one child who was also active in the tower.

In room 11 the EMF sweep produced no anomalies but in this room, the dowsing picked up the sleepy residue of a man who had died of natural causes in 1478. The guest medium felt the presence of an adult female who had died a brutal death, this time getting the name 'Abby' or 'Abigail'. The medium's skin temperature began to fluctuate between 25 and 30°C, an unnatural change in an essentially sealed room! The dowser picked up on Abby too, and found that she'd died in 1747 at the age of 47. At this point, the medium's temperature dropped to 22°C, and she began to feel worried and confused. Again, no records have been found to confirm the existence of Abby.

In room 17, where the medium and the dowser both picked up on a woman in pain as well as a mischievous child, there were no EMF anomalies, but the temperature survey picked up a 6°C fluctuation around the medium and the camcorder refused to focus for no apparent reason. Later, another vigil was held in room 17, with a lock-off camcorder set running. Again, the EMF picked up nothing, but I did get a peculiar light anomaly that doesn't appear to be dust or an insect on digital photography. We also experienced batteries draining during dowsing, when one of the torches dimmed to almost nothing – it was fine again when we left the room. Several of the team tried dowsing in that room and found a mischievous child, again accompanied by temperature fluctuations of up to 7°C. Two people saw visible shadows flashing past.

The bar had proved empty of activity (well, once the wedding guests had finished for the night!) and so staff had locked it. Interesting then that at 5.03am, crashing noises and the distinct sound of movement was heard inside by three team members.

The restaurant, on the other hand, seemed to change its mind as the night when on as to whether or not it was going to play! At the very beginning of the night, two team members had gone in and one of them had seen a moving light and felt something 'blowing' on her ear. However, by the time the first vigil was held in there (near midnight), there was little activity in evidence. EMF and EVP surveys gave no results, and pendulum dowsing proved fruitless, almost as if anything there had moved on. At 3am the team chanced their luck again, with lock-off camcorders and photographic surveys of the dining areas, and while neither EMF or EVP pro-

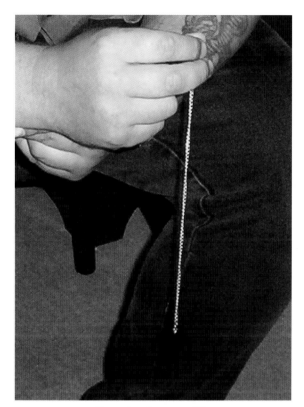

Dowsing in room 17.

duced any results there are at least three 'orbs' on digital camera from this period. The temperature of one of the team members dropped by 6°C and she reported a 'shiver', though no sources of draughts were identified.

At 4am, the final vigil in this area took place with next to no results, except a slight reading on the EMF meter in one of the alcoves which neither of the previous vigils had detected. Anomaly or natural effects of a power surge? It's impossible to tell.

No other activity was recorded during the investigation at Otterburn Tower Hotel, barring the guest medium again identifying the child in the entrance lobby, and the female presence heading towards the dining room. Different vigils with different team members corroborated each other in more than once instance, though of course research into the names and dates has proved inconclusive.

So is the hotel haunted? From the results of the investigation it seems that there is certainly something, or someone in evidence. Perhaps when you visit you'll have a chance to meet the Grey Lady and her mischievous child yourself...

What do you think?

The investigator felt there was a presence nearby. The two light anomalies above were picked up by the digital camera in the restaurant. They appear to be solid and non-transparent.

13. MURDER MOST HORRID

Case Study 30th January 2004
The Schooner Hotel, Alnmouth

Alnmouth, a picturesque Northumbrian village on the coast just over four miles from Alnwick, has a rich and rather varied history. It was founded in 1150 as a 'new town' by the Normans, though there may have been a church there by the 7th century. By 1208 it was an established trade port specialising in grain transport, but in 1336 the village was almost destroyed by maruading Scots and then in 1348 the Black Death attacked what was left of the population. The disease was possibly brought to the village aboard one of the trade vessels.

Recovery was slow, but Alnmouth eventually reached the peak of its prosperity in the 17th and 18th centuries, again becoming an important seaport in the North East. The 1750s saw the construction of the 'corn road' which stretched from Hexham to Alnmouth. Smuggling was a way of life in Alnmouth during these years, only partly curtailed by the building of the customs house. Unfortunately, on Christmas Eve 1806 there was a tremendous storm that changed the course of the River Aln, effectively making the harbour less accessible for anchorage

and beginning the decline of Alnmouth trade by sea. Sea-trade finally all but stopped when the railway was built in the mid-19th century, and if it wasn't for the tourists that the trains brought, the village might well have declined further.

The Schooner Hotel, now a listed building, is said to have been built in the 1600s at the height of Alnmouth's prosperity and, perhaps more importantly, its smuggling past. It has played host to many famous people, including King George III, fighter pilot Douglas Bader and writer Charles Dickens, and legends have grown up about a smugglers' tunnel leading

The Schooner Hotel, on the left, c.1890.

from the cellars down to the Alnmouth beaches.

In more recent years, the Schooner has developed a strong reputation as a place of paranormal activity, earning the title of 'Most Haunted Hotel in Britain' in 2002. Investigation by Living TV's Most Haunted programme certainly boosted that reputation. With ghost nights now being a regular social event at the Schooner, this standing is unlikely to change in the near future.

In March 2003 North East Ghosthunters experienced an 8°C temperature drop in room 28, as well as inexplicable noises, feelings of being watched, and a rather peculiar light anomaly, about the size of a golfball, was caught on tape as it passed between two of the investigators. TAPS (The Answers People Seek), another North East investigation group, investigated the hotel in June 2004 and recorded many orbs on digital camera as well as severe battery drains from cameras and camcorders, especially in the back kitchen corridor. The team also suffered from strange emotional outbursts, found a number of coldspots and one investigator got the fright of his life when he heard a disembodied voice speaking directly into his ear.

Several members of staff at the Schooner have experienced paranormal phenomena on a regular basis. An ex-member of staff remembers an investigation in November 2003 when a team member in room 17 felt as though someone had his hands around her throat and was trying to choke her. My informant had felt this sensation outside the same room two weeks earlier. Another man emerged from room 17 with two long scratch marks down his face. He was certain he hadn't done it himself, although he did remember a burning sensation on his cheek halfway through the vigil.

On another occasion my informant was cleaning room 30. She and a colleague were discussing ghosts – the colleague insisting that ghostly experiences were the product of an overactive imagination – when they heard taps running in the adjoining bathroom. On investigation the bathroom was empty – in fact anyone entering or leaving the bathroom would have had to walk past the two cleaners. Finally, on another investigation, my informant was pushed off a bed by an unseen hand. Her partner, who was sitting beside her, felt something brush past him as she fell.

On 30 January 2004, several members of Otherworld North East, including myself, joined an investigation at the Schooner hosted by Ghost Haunted North East.

When Ghost Haunted's medium arrived he picked up on a voice saying 'Christian perfection' outside the hotel, and felt there was an echo of activity dating from the 1700s in the courtyard.

My group headed off to room 20, and passing by the Foxton Wing of the Schooner (the only section of the hotel without any stories of paranormal activity!) the medium picked up on a spirit insisting on darkness, as he didn't like the light. At this point there were no temperature, EMF or radio frequency anomalies, and unfortunately as far as I know, no anomalies appeared on camera.

We reached the foot of the steps leading up to the room 20 corridor, to be met by what can only be described as a very forbidding atmosphere. Though there were no breezes, the ambient air temperature was fluctuating by 3°C, and the medium decided that it would be best if he went up the stairs alone. A few minutes later, he came back down and requested that the group leave room 20 till later on in the night – specifically 2am – as an unpleasant spirit had confronted him and threatened any women in the group.

Twelve minutes later, the group was standing in the corridor outside room 15, where the medium picked up on the spirit of a Royal Air Force pilot with a limp and a liking for card games. He added that the pilot had a friend who also visited the Schooner, and whose name began with 'D'. Could the spirit's friend have been the World War II fighter pilot Douglas Bader? Unfortunately, the instruments picked up no anomalies during this time, and the medium's external temperature held steady at 22°C.

Around midnight we entered the corridor below the kitchens. A video camera had been locked off in the corridor because mysterious footsteps had been reported there, but the medium felt a strong urge to see for himself. Soon after arriving he appeared to go into a trance and his temperature started to fluctuate by 10°C – highly unnatural! His breathing became strained, and he doubled over, as if held in a chokehold. It took four members of the team to break the trance, and the medium was taken out of the corridor to recover. At this point, the ambient air temperature was fluctuating by 4°C, and there was a highly charged atmosphere, rather like the feeling immediately before a thunderstorm. Much later, the medium suggested that the entity's name was Mallum, and that in life he had been a murderer or an executioner.

Moving on to room 2, the medium picked up on the spirit of a Jonathan Bainbridge, who claimed to have killed a man named Franklin who owed him £15. He said that the incident had occurred at the Tailor's Tavern. During this communication the medium's temperature fluctuated by 5°C. Later historical research showed that there had once been a Tailor's Arms Inn in Alnmouth, but no Tailor's Tavern.

At 1am, we entered the infamous room 28, said to be one of the primary centres of activity at the Schooner, where our medium described the presence of a 'Grey Lady'. He thought she might have been a matron or housekeeper who looked after children. He also said that the real reported activity probably came from a nearby room, which had originally formed part of what was now room 28.

With negative feelings in many of the rooms, entering room 4 was like a breath of fresh air. It felt light and cheerful, and the medium picked up on two homely spirits whom he identified as Lillian Jones and her husband Robert. They gave the group advice about personal matters, including a good recipe for gingerbread! My camera refused to focus when I tried to take photographs of the spot where the medium said Lillian was standing, and there was a temperature anomaly 5°C colder than the rest of the room. However, at the time of writing, no records of a Lillian or Robert Jones associated with the Schooner have been found.

At 2am we kept our appointment with room 20 in the hope that the spirit there would show itself in some way. Temperature readings in the room were averaging between 12.5 and 16°C, though this might have had something to do with airflow from the open loft entrance. Sitting quietly in the room, the medium and one of the other investigators started to feel cold and shivery, and quite suddenly the medium's temperature dropped from 23 to 19°C. He said that he felt as though a weight was pressing down on his shoulders. We tried pendulum dowsing but with no results, and one of the other investigators attempted to provoke any spirit present into doing something, but to no avail. Slightly disappointed, at 3am we moved on to room 7, which felt warm and inviting. However, after only two minutes I felt I was being watched from the doorway, and photographed two 'orbs' above one of the other investigators. Again, we tried pendulum dowsing without results. At 3.35am we decided to try to provoke a reaction. At this point one team member's temperature started to fluctuate between 18.5 and 24.5°C and she felt nervous and very shaky. I started to get responses from dowsing, but as soon as the cameras were turned in the direction of the pendulum, it stopped moving.

Since the investigation on 30 January, Ghost Haunted have returned to the Schooner several times to run Ghost Watch Nights there, and have experienced further activity in the hotel, mostly light anomalies and inexplicable events such as a kettle switching on and boiling by itself. Dark shadows have been seen in the back kitchen corridor that Mallum is said to haunt, and at least one investigator has found himself fleeing the corridor outside room 20, without being able to say why afterwards.

The Schooner's room 28. Any strange lights could be the results of the infra red light affecting the camera lens.

The Schooner corridors.

So does the building deserve its reputation? The investigation was extremely interesting, though of course it is frustrating not to be able to find any of the names delivered by Ghost Haunted's medium. The temperature fluctuations (which only occurred during periods of 'activity') also seemed to indicate an external influence on the environment, and the atmosphere in some of the rooms was thick enough to cut with a knife. Couple that with the experiences of staff and the thousands (literally) of sightings by guests at the hotel as well as the results of other investigations there, it is pretty safe to say that in the Schooner Hotel, you're probably never alone when you get a touch of the shivers!

14. A Hermit's Tale

Warkworth

According to local legend, the banks of the River Coquet by Warkworth Castle, just down the coast from Alnmouth, are haunted by the quiet spectre of a young hermit who lived in a cave nearby. Once a knight who fought against the Scots, the young man mistook his own brother for the enemy in battle and killed him. After the tragedy he devoted the rest his life to solitary prayer. Since that day, the ghostly figure of the hermit has been seen by the river, atoning for his misdeed and grieving for his brother.

The hermitage is cut into the rock upstream from the castle, and visitors to the small site often feel moments of sadness, nausea or even bouts of sudden fear and panic … perhaps a memory of the man who once made the hermitage his home?

The Hermitage at Warkworth around 1900.

TYNE & WEAR

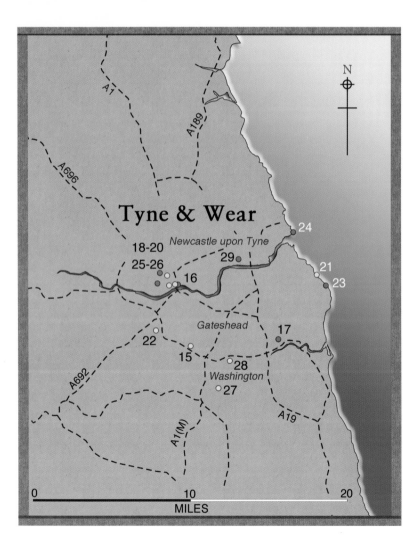

15. ANGEL BELOW

Case Study 6 August 2004
The Angel View Inn, Gateshead

The Angel View Inn, formerly the Old Barn, at Eighton Banks, Gateshead, overlooks Anthony Gormley's sculpture Angel of the North. The inn was originally built as farmhouse and stables. The stonework, layout and form of the old buildings can clearly be seen, along with the old preserved pulley system for lifting bales of hay into the hayloft above the stables.

Legends tell of a young farm-girl killed in the stables when a horse took fright, kicking her in the face. Since then the spirit of the girl, said to be 'faceless', has been seen wandering the corridors and some of the rooms of the inn, sometimes carrying milk churns. The spirit of a female child has also been reported running between the kitchens and the toilets on the ground floor, and a strange shadow has been seen by the bar.

So far, the evidence is as follows. Staff have been alarmed by strange sounds in the dead of night; guests have complained of the sound of automatic fans being turned on in the early hours of the morning in adjacent rooms, only to be told that the room in question was empty; there are also reports of doors being opened and closed, objects moved mysteriously and of course the feeling of being watched, especially from the windows overlooking the inner courtyard. 'Orbs' have been caught on video cameras and blasts of cold air have been felt when entering rooms. Quite a tally of phe-

The Angel View Inn at dawn, after an eventful investigation.

nomena for the Angel View to live up to!

On 6 August 2004, Otherworld North East arrived at the inn to investigate the mysterious activity. There was a wedding reception that night, so the investigation didn't get underway until 12.30am. The nine-strong team divided into three groups and moved around the building all through the night, trying for maximum coverage.

A trigger object was set in the conference room, and a temperature and EMF survey performed at 12.30am but neither survey produced any results. Initial attempts at pendulum dowsing also proved fruitless, but at 12.50am the pendulum started to move, indicating a female presence. The dowser felt the chain was being pulled so hard it was slipping from her fingers. The dowsing indicated a three-year-old child named 'Bo' who was playing with the team, and who claimed she wasn't alone in the room. At 2am, a camcorder was set, and a temperature and EMF survey carried out, while one of the investigators reported an 'orb' shooting across the room. At 2.08am, dowsing was attempted again, with no results though one observer's surface body temperature began to fluctuate between 27 and 32°C, and the EMF meter gave a slight chirping response. Ten minutes later, the pendulum started to move, again picked up a female, this time someone who had worked in the building, was aged 23 or 24 and who said that though she wasn't a milkmaid, she did carry milk and had shown herself to people in the inn doing precisely that. Unfortunately she was unable to spell her name, and when she was questioned about the year of her death, the dowsing stopped. Another dowser took over, and after a few minutes picked up on the young woman, indicating that she'd died as the result of an accident in the 1850s. At 2.45am, the young woman was replaced by a strong male spirit, named 'David Baahn', aged 45 and of Germanic origin.

In the main bar the first vigil took place at 3.35am, with no temperature or EMF changes. One of the team thought he could feel a female presence close to the group, so dowsing was tried. It picked up a little girl, who said she was the same child that had been in the conference room, this time spelling her name 'Deborah' (perhaps 'Bo' was a pet name). Deborah said there was a male spirit with her, who was 45 years old – the age of David Baahn. Two teams, who hadn't discussed their findings with each other, had gained the same result. At 4.19am one of the team saw a dark shadow pass by the bar, in exactly the place that staff had seen the shadow on previous occasions.

In the restaurant, things had started off well with initial EMF sweeps picking up no anomalies. 'Orbs' were seen on camcorder, and at the same time the EMF meter picked up a good reading next to ladies' toilets. One of the investigators felt a small breeze. Dowsing picked up on one male and three female spirits in the building. At 1.22am the dowser's surface body temperature changed by 4°C, and the male presence was 'pushed aside' by a female who claimed to have lived at the inn but not worked there, and who had died of natural causes. Further EMF tests and ultrasound readings were taken at 1.50am, but no anomalies were present. At 2am, the group picked up on a male who was either 45 or 46, and one of the

Inside the inn.

team felt something tug on the torch clipped to her belt. At 5.10am, dowsing picked up on a female aged 24 (a different team once again confirming the results from the conference room) who had worked in the building until her death.

In the function room, where the spirit of the little girl has been seen several times by the staff, there were no EMF fluctuations and the temperature remained constant, though pendulum dowsing picked up a girl, aged 7, who only gave the letter 'I' for her name. During the dowsing an unidentified noise was heard by the team.

There was more dowsing in room 9, where the team picked up on a male, aged 46, who claimed that he wouldn't show himself as he disliked one of the team members! However, when it was suggested that the investigator in question could leave the room, the reply came that the spirit was just playing games. One of the investigators heard the sound of heavy breathing and both he and one other team member saw a light flash twice across the wall, where no rational explanation for the light could be found.

At 2am in room 14, the team picked up on a male in his late forties who seemed unwilling to talk. However by 4am, the investigators picked up on David, who claimed to have followed them from the conference room. He was asked if he was aware of a little girl in the inn, and when asked to spell her name the pendulum constantly repeated the letters 'b' and 'e' over and over again. At 4.20am, the pendulum picked up on a female who had been murdered, sustaining a fatal injury to her head, specifically her face. Perhaps this ties in with the stories of a faceless girl seen around the place. When asked to spell her name, the pendulum spelt 'Deb' before all other contact was lost.

A significant feature of the investigation at the Angel

View Inn was the repeat of the name 'Deb' or 'Deborah' and the constant presence of a man aged 45-46 picked up by different team members who hadn't collaborated or shared notes during the investigation. It does seem likely that the Angel View Inn is haunted by memories of the past.

The outside staircase, where a ghostly girl has been reported on numerous occasions.

16. Away with the Spirits

The Cooperage, Newcastle

The Cooperage, on Newcastle Quayside, is one of the oldest timber-framed buildings in the city, dating back to the 15th century. At various periods the building has been a private house, a warehouse, and of course a cooperage (where barrels were made). It became a public house and restaurant in 1973. It is the focus of a number of ghostly tales, making it one of the region's most haunted pubs. Many members of staff have reported hearing footsteps on the old staircases when they know they're alone in the building, and both staff and customers have mentioned seeing something out of the corner of their eye which vanishes when they look to see what it is. Four different apparitions have also been seen in the pub: a young blonde haired girl, a man looking out of a window, a faint spectre of a woman in the restaurant and a figure that is said to change colour like a chameleon. The dark alleyway by the side of the Cooperage is thought to be haunted by the ghost of a cooper who was waylaid by the press-gang in the 16th century: when he refused to be taken to the ship, they put his eyes out and killed him. Since that day his ghost has been seen stumbling in blind agony around the site of his murder.

The Cooperage, 1931.

17. Brownie or Ghost?

Hylton Castle, Near Sunderland

Hylton Castle is no stranger to tales of things that go bump in the night; the most famous or infamous of these stories tells of the mischievous gremlin known as the 'Cauld Lad', a brownie-type sprite that was said to run riot through the Castle frightening milk maids, wailing and … tidying up! According to tradition if anything was left in a mess in the kitchens and hall, the Cauld Lad would tidy it, but if it was left in order, he would throw things around in a fit of annoyance. Eventually, the castle servants got sick of his antics, and left a new hood and cloak out for him one night. He was never seen again.

Often confused with the brownie legends, are the ghost tales of Hylton Castle. Reports of ghostly activity were extremely common until the beginning of the 18th century, with tales of horrifying sounds and screams and furniture being moved around the castle – so much so that apparently a priest was called to perform an exorcism. The activity, unaffected by the exorcism, seemed to draw to a close soon after a body of a young boy was found when a pond near the castle was drained in 1703. So was it the ghost of this boy that had haunted the castle? It seems that the activity had started soon after 1609. On 3 July that year, a coroner's inquest took place following the alleged murder of a stable boy, Roger Skelton, at the hands of the then Baron, Sir Robert Hylton. The story goes that the Baron had found the boy asleep in the straw in the stables when he should have been saddling a horse; in a fit of rage, Robert Hylton took a pitch fork and killed the lad. However, all charges were dropped against the Baron because no body was found. From that moment the ghost of the murdered boy was said to haunt Hylton Castle until his body was finally discovered and buried decently almost one hundred years after his death.

Hylton Castle in 1936.

18. THE MYSTERIOUS ETHEL

John Lewis, Eldon Square, Newcastle upon Tyne

Bainbridge's, now John Lewis, is a Newcastle department store with over 150 years of history. However, the tales of supernatural activity are not associated with the firm's old premises in Market Street but with Eldon Square, just after the move there in the 1970s.

Bainbridge's ghost is a Grey Lady, quite literally a grey-haired old lady often seen in the restaurant.

The spectre was reported by a waitress who noticed her sitting alone at a table, hat pulled over her eyes and coat buttoned to the top. Suddenly the lady vanished without a trace!

The ghost of the little Grey Lady was seen so often that she was nicknamed 'Ethel' by the Bainbridge catering partners. One of her other favourite 'haunts' was the catering partner cloakrooms. One of the chefs was having a shower when his friends decided to play a prank and turn out the lights. When the chef turned around he could make out a white shape moving across the room. He was shocked when his friends adamantly denied that they'd staged the 'ghost'.

Soon afterwards, another member of staff became aware of a little old lady dressed in grey beside her in the staff cloakrooms. Thinking that the lady must be lost, she turned to speak to her, but the Grey Lady had vanished.

'Ethel' was also regularly seen in the Counting House on a Saturday morning, as well as in the shoe department. Her hunched figure was glimpsed by members of staff on their way out of the stockroom, but she always vanished a moment later.

However, sightings of the Grey Lady began to diminish, until in 1988, the *Bainbridge Chronicle* reported, 'The Grey Lady has not been seen for many years now'.

Theories about ghosts abound, but if people can leave memories of themselves when they die, who was the Grey Lady? The Restaurant and Shoe Departments are almost directly above Prudhoe Street where the Prudhoe Street Mission used to be. Perhaps Ethel was disturbed by the commotion of Bainbridge's hectic arrival and, once she'd checked that her new neighbours met with her approval, she was content to let Bainbridge be...

Prudhoe Street and the Prudhoe Street Mission, long buried beneath Eldon Square. Could Ethel have emanated from here to Bainbridge's?

19. EDUCATED ENTITIES

Case Study 12 December 2003
Literary and Philosophical Society, Newcastle

The Literary and Philosophical Society building is between Bolbec Hall and Neville Hall on Westgate Road, just down from Central Station. It was purpose-built for the Society, the foundation stone being laid in September 1822, and the building opening for use three years later in July 1825. In 1893 it was gutted by a fire which destroyed the roof, the floor and many of the 35,000 books: nearly 10,000 were destroyed completely, just over 7,000 badly damaged and most of the rest suffered damage to their covers and binding. The building was refurbished and finally opened again in October 1894.

It is associated with a number of ghosts, the most common phenomenon being the sound of phantom pages being turned in the ground floor reading room, sometimes accompanied by the sight of a shadowy figure. It is said that one of the Society's old librarians, T.H. Marr, still walks the rooms and corridors he loved. On numerous occasions, staff have also noted a door in the basement area opening and closing itself, and many visitors, in particular women, have found the basement book store uncomfortable when there alone. There is also at least one report of the furniture rearranging itself overnight in one of the lecture rooms!

On the cold, wet night of 12 December 2003, the Otherworld North East team investigated the alleged hauntings, with simple electromagnetic, temperature and photographic equipment. Baseline tests were carried out the evening before. The tests had produced a strange light anom-aly in the main library area, a sporadic electromagnetic fluctuation in the ground floor reading room and a constant low reading in one section of the basement book store, so the team was keen to see what was there.

The investigation started at 10.30pm with a walkaround by the team's medium. In the depths of the building, he picked up on a James Scott and a Reverend Turner in the

basement book store, with Turner again appearing in the adjacent boiler room, as well as a Henry Stapleton. He also said there was a Thomas present, possibly a chemist, who had followed the group down there from the rooms above, merely out of curiosity. He claimed that a spirit walked through the firedoors, though he couldn't work out a name or form at that point, but the library staff present were able to confirm that this was the door that had been seen opening and closing by itself. At the same time one of the investigators got a severe case of the shivers and said she could smell burning paper.

At 11.08pm, the medium picked up on a Charles Bigge in the main lecture room, as well as a Reverend John H. Bruce, and commented that a lot of clergy seemed to be associated with the building. He also got a 'Hugh' but no surname. By this time names were coming to the medium so quickly that it was confusing. He noted there was an Elizabeth present, who he identified as Elizabeth Spence-Watson, as well as a gentleman named Swan. Another man had strong connections with China; the staff present suggested might have been Robert Morris, though the medium couldn't confirm the name.

In the corridor outside the lecture room, by the reading room, the medium found a lot of residual energy. He sensed that footsteps would often be heard walking through this area.

In the reading room, he noted the pres-ence of two individuals, Ruth Dodds, a strong woman who campaigned for women's rights, and Richard Welford. He said that people would be able to hear the sounds of pages being turned in that room when no-one else was present.

In the main library on the first floor, the medium identified Reverend William Turner again, describing him as pompous. There was another Reverend with a name sounding like 'Bells' or 'Belzer'. Ruth Dodds seemed to have followed us, as had Thomas. The medium suggested that things might be moved around the library, but none of the staff present could confirm that.

The Lit and Phil around 1930. Visitors will find the furnishings little changed.

On the top floor, the medium felt the area closest to the door by the oval table in the Committee Room contained a negative presence. This confused him as he said it seemed not to have a connection with the building, but dated back to a far earlier time. He identified the presence as a witchfinder who had sent 210 people to the stake. He thought that objects might be be moved around in the room. As the presence made him feel unwell, the group decided to take a small break before starting the investigation proper.

The first team entered the boiler room at 1.14am and found little activity except a few minor temperature fluctuations. One of the team did feel hands on her shoulders for a few seconds. However, the atmosphere intensified at 3am when the second group entered. An EMF and temperature survey recorded no anomalies, but during the photo survey one of the team caught a blue-purple haze above the firedoor which had been seen opening and closing itself – a photograph which it has not so far been possible to explain. Three bangs were heard five minutes later, and the medium faintly picked up on the name 'Armstrong'. Dowsing brought no results at first, but soon one of the team was shocked by an extremely strong pull on the pendulum. The results indicated the presence of a child named Aimee, but after the

The photograph of a mist above the boiler room door taken by Danny Jones. Right, a computer enhancement of the mist.

name had been spelled out contact ceased completely.

The basement book store is a peculiar area of the building, reached by several narrow corridors, with noise from the boiler room next door reverberating through it. The first team had problems focusing camcorders here, and at least one member of the team felt he was being watched. The temperature fluctuated between 19° and 25°C. Though pendulum dowsing gave no results, at 1.38am the motion sensors in the main store corridor were triggered without explanation.

At 3.30am, the second vigil was held in the bookstore, where the team medium almost immediately saw a light anomaly move down the corridor where the sensors had been triggered. I walked down the corridor myself, taking a temperature survey with no results. However, as I returned towards the door, I was surprised to feel something tugging on my trouser leg, though I was alone, and nowhere near anything that could have snagged on the material.

We settled down to observe the corridor. The medium reported a red streak of light down the corridor at 3.50am, and when one of the team sat half way down the passage she reported a 'fluttering' sound and noted moving shadows around the doorways. At this point, the medium identified a spirit called Marr (and thought his first name might have been Thomas) who often wandered the book store checking on those working down there.

It was at 4.17am that things in the store began to get a little more strange, with the batteries of the camcorder beginning to drain very quickly. At the same time the medium again saw the red light anomaly. Everyone in the group started to feel uneasy, and our temperatures were fluctuating by up to 8°C … and at that point the camcorder and the torch batteries died simultaneously!

Looking down the book store corridor during one of the vigils.

I felt a distinct pressure on my shoulders and neck, as if someone was pressing hands firmly down on them, though when the medium asked for the 'spirit' to back off, the feeling vanished, only to be replaced by nausea also reported by another member. Four minutes later, the torch came back on by itself, though it required a battery change. With the atmosphere lifting, a digital dictaphone was set running and the group left the room.

The first vigil in the reading room on the ground floor was very quiet, with only minor dowsing results, accompanied by a 6°C surface body temperature drop in the dowser. The pendulum indicated a female presence, but little else, and one of the team got the impression of something present with a dislike of men. Dowsing identified another child as 'Emily Braithwaite'. Sadly, none of the trigger objects set up in the Reading Room moved, though a lock-off video camera did show a number of moving 'orbs' or light anomalies.

In the first floor library, at 11.15pm, one of the team members was startled by something tugging hard at the chair in which she was sitting. At 1am the medium identified a spirit of a little girl, 'Katie Hewitt', in the vicinity, so maybe she was playing with the chair for attention! The temperature in the library fluctuated by about 3°C through the night, but dowsing got no results. However, at 1.05am the medium picked up on a Thomas Brockett who was looking for his favourite book on the shelves, and at 1.21am the medium and I both heard distinct footsteps behind us, though no-one was there. Later on in the morning, a moving light anomaly was caught on night vision video next to the clock in the library offshoot area.

Through a small door off the library is the ladies' room, which was first investigated at 12.30am with no EMF or temperature results, and fruitless attempts at dowsing. The medium attempted to make some contact, but although his temperature fluctuated between 21 and 28°C, there were no inci-

dents. He said that they were being watched by a male presence, but they were there at the wrong time, and that the room was probably only active later in the morning. To test this idea, the second vigil took place there at 2.50am, with the temperature survey picking up a fluctuation in the southwest corner of the room, bouncing between 21 and 27°C.

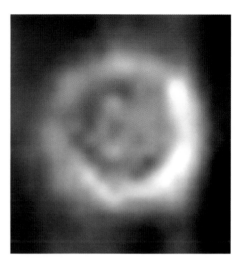

Computer enhanced anomaly photographed just after hearing footsteps in the first floor library.

With this in mind, the group started dowsing at 3am, with strong results, indicating a female presence, possibly a Ruth, who had been married with three children, and had worked at the society. She seemed unhappy that the group was there, but didn't really want them to go. Soon after, a door slammed shut in the library (possibly one of the staff). Communication was lost but the air temperature continued to fluctuate between 20.5 and 25.9°C making the group feel cold and shivery.

On the top floor and balcony, the medium picked up on Charles Bigge again, this time in the committee room, feeling he had been an important man, a sheriff or mayor. The trigger objects set near the 'negative' presence felt earlier showed no movement, though at 1.48am, one member of the group developed sudden toothache while something caught the eye of one of the investigators – photographs were taken and a large light anomaly was photographed in the air above the tooth-aching investigator's head!

At 3.30am, dowsing indicated the presence of a Scottish male from the 13th century, though why he should be in a room built 600 years later was never explained! During the dowsing one of the investigators became very cold down one side of his body, his right side measuring 30°C and his left side 23°C. An EMF survey of the room picked up a high reading on three of the chairs around the table (there had been no reading beforehand), the scope of the readings almost seeming to map people sitting in the chairs.

The balcony produced no results, though 12 photographs taken on digital camera simply vanished from the memory card. One photograph of the view down into the library area caught two bright 'orbs' that appear to be three-dimensional in shape, and about the size of a tennis ball.

Out of 17 names given by the medium during the investigation, eight can be identified at this time, but it must be noted that these eight are in the public record and can viewed on the Society web-pages.

With many of the classic symptoms of a haunted building, the Literary and Philosophical Society of Newcastle upon Tyne is a wonderful place to visit, but just remember to check that those footsteps behind you, or the pages turning in the next alcove do indeed belong to a living, breathing person!

A light anomaly caught on camera in the committee room just as movement caught the eye of one investigator, and another developed toothache. Below, the anomaly enhanced.

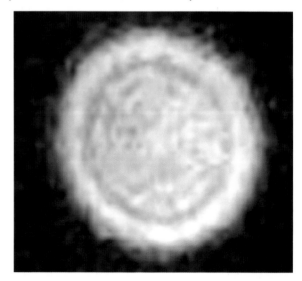

20. Keeping with Tradition

Case Studies 22 August 2003, 27 February 2004
Castle Garth, Newcastle upon Tyne

The first thing that many people notice about the 'new castle' of Newcastle upon Tyne is that Castle Garth is cut quite neatly in two by a railway viaduct, complete with working railway line! On one side sits the Keep and on the other the Black Gate; the two were divided in 1847 to accommodate the increasingly heavy use of railways in the industrial town. These days, the Keep stands amid the bustle of modern Newcastle, its key role in the history and development of the north known by few.

Until recent years it also seemed that centuries of bloodshed had left no mark on the building, with only the legend of the Poppy Girl haunting its chambers, though the source of that legend, which tells the haunting of the Garrison Room by a young woman, has never been verified by historians. Strangely, over the last couple of years in particular, odd sights and sounds have been heard in the Keep with such regularity that one of the staff has even bought himself nightvision camcorder equipment in an attempt to find the source of the ghostly goings-on. Perhaps the activity was sparked by recent renovation.

So what events lie in the Keep's past that could

The Keep in the snow … not an anomaly in sight!

have rooted lost souls in the corridors and halls? Looking at the Keep it is often difficult to imagine nearly 1000 years of political machinations and bloody warfare.

The castle was built in 1080 on ground that, according to archaeological evidence, held traces of Iron Age agriculture, a small Roman fort named Pons Aelius, and a Saxon cemetery and monastery referred to by historians as Monkchester. The first castle, thought to have been constructed of earth and timber, was commissioned by Robert Curthose, a son of William the Conqueror, who had been sent north to wage war with King Malcolm of Scotland. Malcolm had invaded Northumbria a year before, but probably found little left to ransack after the 'harrying of the North' when William had put the area to sword and flame post-Conquest. Six years after the castle was built the Domesday Book was completed, but neither Northumberland nor Durham were included due to the terrible devastation.

And so began the history of a castle that came to be used as a strategic and political gamepiece by kings of England and Scotland. To detail all of the intrigues and history fully would require a small book all of its own! The castle first saw military action in 1095 when William the Conqueror's son William Rufus besieged it in a dispute over the succession. Forty years later, the Scots under King David I invaded and captured Newcastle, as well as Norham, Wark and Alnwick. The north remained under Scottish control until 1156.

Between the years 1168 and 1178 King Henry I ordered the castle to be rebuilt in stone. Midway through the construction William of Scotland invaded Northumberland again but was captured and imprisoned in the unfinished 'new castle'. He was shipped off to Rouen and ransomed for £4,000 on the condition that he give up all claim to Northumberland. Unfortunately for King William, the route his party took back to Scotland went via Newcastle … whereupon he found that the inhabitants of the town were not as forgiving as the English monarchy! The mob fell on the royal party, and though William just escaped, most of the royal escort lost their lives in the vengeful attack.

Thirty-five years later the Scots attempted to reclaim Northumberland, and in 1213, Newcastle prepared to defend itself from the castle walls with an order of over one thousand jars of lime for throwing at the enemy.

In 1244, after years of fighting, Henry III's daughter, Margaret, married the King of Scotland's son, Alexander, in a political move. The Keep's barbican, the Black Gate, was built between 1247 and 1250, and the subsequent years saw major repairs and eventually the start of the Town Walls under the reign of Edward I in 1272.

And then, in 1296, along came William Wallace, the Scottish army under his command plunging into Northumberland, but wisely avoiding the heavily defended Newcastle. A year later, Wallace won the Battle of Stirling and marched south, being turned away from Newcastle. But Wallace's connection with Newcastle does not end there: in 1298 after his execution, his right arm was displayed on one of the bridges crossing the Tyne, and other 'undisclosed' parts of his anatomy were put on public display on the walls of the Keep!

In 1323, after the Battle of Bannockburn and a peace treaty with Scotland, another gruesome public display appeared on the walls of the castle – this time one of the quarters of Andrew de Hartcla, first Earl of Carlisle.

So much for treaties. In the mid-14th century the Scots

under King David rampaged south again and unsuccessfully besieged Newcastle. Four years later, the Scots were defeated at the Battle of Neville's Cross, and David was imprisoned in the Keep.

The year 1400 saw a big political change for Newcastle, when Henry IV granted a charter that separated the town from Northumberland, essentially making it into a county in its own right. A significant exclusion to this was the castle and its lands, which oddly remained part of Northumberland. The Keep became Northumberland's county gaol and Newgate, within the town wall, became a gaol for the town authorities.

Between 1400 and 1415, Newcastle witnessed a rebellion against Henry IV by Northumberland's Percy family, and predictably part of the quartered body of Harry Hotspur, son of Henry Percy (Earl of Northumberland) was displayed as a warning on the castle walls. Continuing the grisly tradition the head of Sir Thomas Grey of Wark was later displayed over the gate at Newcastle after he was executed for treason.

Immune from local authority power, many criminals took refuge inside the castle yard, safe from prosecution by a matter of feet. In 1589 Queen Elizabeth I brought the 'safe house' to an end and granted the town authorities license to enter the grounds, which might have come as quite a shock to some on the licence's first day! By this time the Keep is reported to be 'old and ruinous', and by 1620 part of the west curtain wall collapsed under the pressure caused by the massive pile of refuse and other not so pleasant deposits!

In 1638, as war approached, the castle was strengthened but that didn't stop the Scots occupying Northumberland and Newcastle in 1640. After a year the English Parliament paid the Scots £300,000 to leave.

Then in 1642 came the Civil War, Royalist Newcastle holding out against the Parliamentarian Scots. It is reported that the mayor, Sir John Marley, used dung from the huge dung and rubbish heap by the Keep to reinforce the castle walls. The castle was duly besieged, bravely defended, and inevitably fell, with Sir John taken prisoner. However, he escaped imprisonment on his way to London, and fled into exile in true Hollywood fashion. It was this siege that gave Newcastle its motto 'Fortiter Defendit Triumphans' ('she bravely defends and triumphs'), awarded by a very impressed Charles I.

By 1732 the castle was once again described as neglected and in 1733, one of the most bizarre incidents in the Keep's history took place. A showman drew a crowd with the announcement that he would wear homemade wings and fly

The Keep in 1790.

from the top of the Keep. However, he became nervous when a huge crowd assembled below and instead strapped the wings to his faithful pack-donkey, somehow pushing the poor beast from the top of the 100-foot tower. Amazingly, the donkey survived the fall, due largely to the unfortunate spectator on whom the beast landed…

By 1734 the Keep had no roof, and the floors had mostly decayed away, the only one in use being the first floor which formed the roof over the county gaol. To add insult to injury, by 1778 the ornate Chapel was being used as a beer cellar and by the end of the 18th century the building had lost all value as a defensible structure. An icehouse had been dug into the south-west corner of the Keep, and a currier (leather worker) had set up his workshop somewhere within the walls. At this point, the Keep's roof was also being used as a cabbage garden, and the authorities started to take notice.

Between 1810 and 1812, Newcastle Corporation purchased the remains of the castle and began to restore it. They decided to fire a cannon from the roof of the Keep at noon each day and on special occasions. Unfortunately on 7 May 1812, John Robson, a gunner, fired a shot from the roof of the Keep and forgot to swab out the cannon before he put in the second shot. The cannon, still hot from the first shot, lit the second charge before he was ready. Poor Robson's right hand was blown off, the impact throwing him from the roof of the Keep. It was noted that firing the cannon often set fire to the densely packaged houses around the Keep… and the practice was hastily discontinued.

It wasn't until the 19 June 1813 that the fully restored Keep was opened to the public, and that same year, after the Peterloo Massacre in Manchester, the 40th Regiment of Fusiliers garrisoned the Keep. However, the regiment saw little trouble in Newcastle and after they left, the Keep continued to be used as a debtors' prison until 1823.

In 1847, the railway viaduct was constructed through Castle Garth, effectively cutting the castle in two. During excavations for the building work human bones and other remains were found near the castle. A year later, the Society of Antiquaries rented the Keep for their museum, library and meeting place, and John Dobson, a celebrated architect, carried out further restoration work. Gas lighting was also

1812, the Keep during restoration.

installed, and then the Keep was once again opened to the public in December 1848.

In 1882, Newcastle became a city, and between 1883 and 1885, the Barbican, or Black Gate was restored and the Society of Antiquaries moved there, though they continued to manage the Keep. A year later, the railway viaduct was widened, creating the effect we see today.

The Keep escaped the ravages of the Second World War, but the years 1939-1945 saw the roof of the Keep being used as a joint fire-warden and air-raid post, and the basement of the Keep as an air-raid shelter.

Most recently, between 1960 and the 1990s the Keep has undergone extensive restoration work, and excavations of the Castle Garth burials were completed in 1992.

Looking at the history of the building it is not difficult to see the potential for paranormal activity, especially if you support the idea that ghosts are created from violence or strong emotions, and then sometimes disturbed by building or other restoration work.

On Hallowe'en, 2002, a local investigation team spent the night in the Keep, hoping to discover evidence of supernatural activity on that supposedly most active of nights – they found nothing, and left disappointed.

By the following summer a night in Newcastle Keep told an entirely different story. On 22 August 2003 Otherworld North East, with UK Ghost Investigators and Ghost Haunted North East, undertook an overnight vigil in the Keep on a warm, windless and balmy night, which made it all the easier to notice the cold sourceless breezes and massive sudden temperature drops.

The old gaol or Garrison Room on the ground floor of the Keep was found to be a potential 'hotspot' of anom-

Newcastle Keep, August 2004.

alous occurrences from the word go, with Ghost Haunted's medium coming into contact with a young woman on the steps of the room claiming to be a victim of rape and murder. Was this the alleged Poppy Girl? To back the medium's claim a small glowing ball of light on the step on which he said she was standing, was captured on digital camera.

He also felt that there was a great deal of information 'recorded' in the room, that he could see a replay of a dozen marching chain-mailed soldiers carrying pikes or halberds, and could sense bodies buried beneath the floor – certainly possible due to the Anglo-Saxon cemetery upon which the Keep was built. Sound recording equipment was later found to have distorted badly in this room, and the temperature at various parts of the night was recorded as dropping significantly over a matter of seconds.

Filming the Garrison Room with night vision camcorder.

The medium was determined to find more details about the girl in the Garrison Room, so his team staked out the room in the hope that she would reappear. Soon after the vigil started, he saw her walking down the steps and across to the fireplace. He described her as a young woman with the name Briony or perhaps Annie. Astonishingly, the air temperature in the path she was 'walking', measured only 14.7°C in comparison to the rest of the room at 25.3°C… an anomaly that was anything but natural!

After 'Briony' vanished, the group stayed in the room, where the medium said he could feel energy building, and recorded more temperature fluctuations, bouncing between 25.3°C and 15.1°C. At the peak of this fluctuation, he claimed to see 30 soldiers in chainmail walk through the room, perhaps another memory of times past being replayed.

Later in the Garrison Room, UK Ghost Investigators' medium picked up on a Jeremiah Kinstone in the condemned cell, and one of the other team members said she could sense another male in the room by the name of Jacob. Some team members had problems with equipment, in particular cameras not focusing or working properly, and others felt breathless with tightness in their chests.

Before the door was blocked up with stone, it would have been possible to walk from the Garrison Room through to the Mezzanine Chamber, another small room that seemed to have a tale to tell and a wish to communicate. This room was very warm and stuffy, and the windows and corridors were checked and found to have little air movement – yet in the early part of the vigil, during initial baseline testing, the investigators felt a breeze blow across their skin, but could find no source. Again, the room proved awkward for recording sound, with lots of static produced, and one of the mediums felt a strong spirit present who he identified the spirit as Jacob Alnwick, a Scottish guard, who really didn't want the team in there! The temperature was fluctuating wildly between 16 and 31.9°C, though no breeze could be felt.

At that point that I started to feel really uncomfortable. I could feel a breeze blowing around me, though no-one else could see or feel it. My temperature was taken and was ranging between 17.1 and 29.4°C. The medium saw a spirit whom he called William standing behind me, and also Jacob marching up the stairs leading out of the chamber – digital photography showed 'orbs' on the steps at that point – but then coming down again shouting 'Out!'.

Knowing that the next group was due, the group left Jacob to it. Interestingly UKGI's medium also picked up on Jacob down there, but found him rather different, a spirit who wanted to be heard, rather than wanting the team out of there! Later, team members felt cold and nervous in the room, and one investigator felt a stabbing pain.

At the other side of the Keep, the Chapel was quite active… perhaps its use as a beer store in the 18th century had angered the spirits! The investigators all independently reported strange clicking noises from near the grave slabs on display, and several reported clothing being tugged by fingers unknown. Dowsing with pendulums indicated the presence of at least one man who had been executed for murder. The

The Mezzanine steps where Jacob Alnwick's spirit is said to prowl.

name 'Andrew' was independently picked up by two different sensitives, and there seemed to be an almost permanent cold spot around the gravestones. When any spirit present was asked to show a sign, a few of the investigators saw flashes of light – in the same place. Immediately on entering the Chapel, Ghost Haunted's medium saw a man in the corner of the room whom he identified as Samuel Peters who had been executed for murder – though he seemed unwilling or unable to tell the medium if he'd been guilty or not. A digital dictaphone was set up though sadly no EVP was recorded.

Moving up to the Great Hall, it is easy to see why many think they're being watched, with two levels of galleries overlooking the room, each filled with shadows. Perhaps that is why three different people reported feeling as though they were being watched, by a woman, from the galleries… but it doesn't really explain why each chose the same gallery.

Moving lights caught on two successive photographs taken in the Great Hall by Paul McDonald, warden at the Keep.

Even more interesting, 'orbs' were caught on night vision video cameras moving swiftly across the Hall like shooting stars – much too fast to be insects or dust particles. A number of very peculiar images were also caught on digital camera, many in the same area where, earlier in the year, another investigative group, Avalon Skies, had photographed a mist which many interpret as possessing human features.

What really sticks in my mind about the Great Hall on that night, was Ghost Haunted's medium saying that at one point there were many people dancing around the investigation team, accompanied by wildly fluctuating temperatures (15.1-26.6°C). At that precise time there was a completely independent report from the group in the Museum Room below the Hall saying they couldn't concentrate due to the 'running' footsteps from the hall above! Coincidence? Or did that group actually hear the ghostly echoes of the dancing men and women that the medium claimed he could see? There was, yet again, a problem with instruments, with batteries being drained and one of the camcorders losing all ability to focus for about three minutes.

Perhaps the strangest and most compelling event of the night was the séance held in the Garrison Room, led by UKGI's medium. As with the majority of séances I have witnessed, nothing really seemed to be happening, and the group was getting ready to give up. Monitored by EMF and temperature gauges, nothing was showing, not even a blip on the meters.

Then Ghost Haunted's medium, who had been observing the experiment, whispered to me that the spirit Briony had entered the room and was observing the séance with interest. At the same time, one of the members of the circle (the seance was held around the central pillar of the Garrison Room, each person holding hands with the next to form an unbroken circle) started to feel unwell and unexpectedly stood up effectively breaking the circle – something which I was later told was a very bad idea. The group moved to close the circle again, but not before Ghost Haunted's medium began pacing, and muttering that Briony wasn't at all pleased! He seemed to follow something moving through the room, until he finally declared that she had now seated herself in the empty

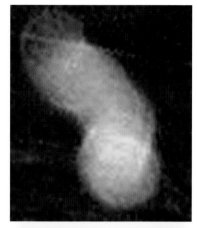

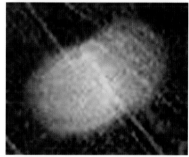

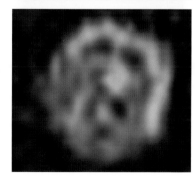

Enhancements of the light anomalies photographed in the Great Hall, on the opposite page.

seat ... the investigators recording the experiment continued to take readings, with no results – until they came to the 'empty' chair when the EMF meter simply went off the scale, as if there was a huge electromagnetic source in the chair itself! The readings lasted only a few moments, but long enough to be recorded, and better yet, after the séance finished, no EMF anomalies could be found anywhere in the Garrison Room, not even the chair itself in which the spirit of Briony had allegedly sat.

With all this activity in mind, the Otherworld North East team, with guests from across the country including members of Ghosts-UK, one of the biggest online paranormal communities in the UK, eagerly awaited the return investigation on February 27th, 2004. At first it seemed that even the weather was against us with the North East seeing the worst blizzard conditions of the winter on that day, but in the end the majority of the planned 30-strong team battled through ice and snowstorms to arrive at the frozen Newcastle Keep. The weather conditions did have some benefits, in that fewer party-goers were on the streets, trains had been cancelled, and sound in general was muffled due to the snow, meaning less sound contamination. It did however mean people had to leave early to avoid being stuck in Newcastle, and also that while standing on the roof of the Keep was certainly refreshing, it played merry hell with the electronic equipment!

Once underway, the rather chilly team started to get results in the chapel almost immediately, with dowsing rods communicating with a female who was frightened of us. No EMF or temperature fluctuations (the temperature of the stonework of the walls averaged 1°C) were recorded and the room felt calm. In an attempt to get more information, the dowser explained to the spirit that the group meant her no harm, whereupon the room felt a little warmer and the rods started to respond to questions, indicating a female who had died in 1656 at the age of 43. Unfortunately, the group was only able to gain the letter 'F' for her surname, which certainly isn't enough for a historical search! Half an hour later more dowsing was performed by a different team member, again picking up a female but this time a 17-year-old born in 1752, who identified herself as 'Barbara'. This time the dowsing was accompanied by an unidentifiable smell and a visible shadow around the pendulum reported by three of the team members. Trigger objects were set up at 1.45am, and a female 'B' was picked up at 2am, accompanied by general atmospheric temperature fluctuations in the chapel, small breezes and a couple of the team members feeling generally nauseous. Over the period of the investigation, the chapel also produced a number of interesting light anomalies both on video and digital camera.

In the Mezzanine Chamber, one of the previous investigation's hotspots, things were quiet when the first team moved in at 11pm, with no EMF or temperature anomalies, and no response from dowsing rods. However, at 11.30pm a low-level EMF reading was taken in the centre of the room that seemed to move towards the stairs then vanish. The next group arrived an hour later, with one team member sitting on the steps and asking for anything present to show itself.

Astonishingly, as he asked for activity, a very large bright light anomaly (probably about five inches across) was captured moving smoothly down the stairs of the Chamber, past the team and towards the blocked-up doorway through to the Garrision Room.

Later, during one of the vigils in the Chamber, there was the feeling of being watched from the top of the stairs, and one of the dowsers reported something flicking her hair while she was standing in the blocked-up doorway alcove.

Through that doorway into the Garrison Room, things were quite active with a number of light anomalies being caught on camera. Some team members felt nauseated and claustrophobic, and it was intensely cold (not really surprising considering the outside weather conditions!). Just after midnight two team members reported a 'horrible laughing sound' accompanied by the feeling that someone was hiding at the top of the stairs next to the condemned cell.

When the next group moved in there at 1.40am, it got even more interesting. The team set up a digital dictaphone, then asked anything present to show itself. At first, there was no response, and then one of the cameramen reported a flicker of light on the bottom step of the flight leading up the stairs to the cell. We asked again and the camcorder picked up a shadow of a figure, moving in profile across the room – everyone in the room was seated and unmoving, so who or what had cast the shadow? The investigation team was unable to come up with a logical explanation for that one …

At 4.15am a moving light anomaly passed across the bottom rail in the condemned cell, and subsequent attempts at photography resulted in two cameras refusing to co-operate. Pendulum dowsing revealed the presence of a male border reiver with the name Clifford, who had died at the age of 28

A photograph taken by Trevor Brown of Avalon Skies of a rather peculiar mist in the Great Hall.

along with five companions. Several team members reported feeling a breeze, though a flame test showed no air movement, and they also reported the sound of 'rasping' breath.

In the Great Hall, things were a lot quieter than they had been on the previous investigation, with minor temperature fluctuations ranging from 4.8-8.5°C and reports of minor activity, such as the feeling of something brushing past one of the team, in the Well Room. Two presences were identified through dowsing, one a female under 30 years old who used to work at the castle, and the other a young male under 20 years old by the name of James.

The Window Room saw trigger object movement when we found that coins we had left there had shifted several inches, and in the Hall itself a crucifix had moved fractionally, though we agreed that such a tiny movement could have been caused by vibration.

Since then, the Castle Keep, now a reported hotspot of paranormal activity with a reputation spreading countrywide, has been the subject of numerous investigations with varying results, many of which concentrate around the Mezzanine Chamber, the Garrison Room and the Great Hall, with further mists pho-

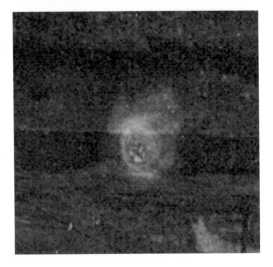

tographed in the Hall and adjoining King's Chamber, and light anomalies caught on camera and camcorder moving down the Mezzanine stairs and taking a right turn through the blocked-up door to the Garrision Room! From a quiet historical monument with little or no alleged paranormal activity, the Keep is rapidly gaining the reputation that there are certain areas of it that the tourist or visitor may not wish to enter alone …

Not just a modern phenomenon – the Well Room in 1910. Just what is the odd light hovering above the well's wooden cover (top picture)? Can you see a face in the enlargement below?

21. A Smuggler's Den

Case Study

Marsden Grotto, 5 December 2003 South Shields

Marsden Grotto is one of the more famously haunted locations in the North East, its name conjuring up images of caves and caverns full of mystery. The Grotto is actually a restaurant cut into the cliff at Marsden Rock in South Shields, and is reputedly home to things that quite literally go bump in the night. The coastline is dotted with small caves that have been used for centuries for smuggling tobacco and other contraband. In 1782 Jack Bates, a quarryman, built a small home for himself and his wife in a cave, using explosives to excavate it, thus gaining himself the nickname 'the Blaster'. The Blaster and his wife lived there happily for a decade, until Jack's death in 1792.

The House in the Cave wasn't inhabited again until 1826, when a local man named Peter Allan moved in and constructed a 15-room public house there, which he later named the Marsden Grotto. Naturally the pub was a great success, especially with the local smugglers, and the Grotto changed hands in the 1840s, passing to Sidney Milnes Hawkes.

There are many tales of ghosts in the Grotto. The most common is that of a smuggler whose colleagues hung him above the main hall to starve to death after some indiscretion. It is said his ghost can still be heard on stormy nights screaming in hunger and terror.

The other well-documented ghost of the Grotto is a dealer in illicit contraband, whose death was witnessed by Peter Allan in the 1840s. The young smuggler was tricked by an undercover Excise officer and realising his mistake tried to

Marsden Grotto.

escape down the beach outside the pub – but the Excise man pulled a pistol and shot him dead. Peter Allan then emptied the smuggler's tankard and uttered the words: 'Let no man drink from this tankard from this day forth lest he be accursed.' He hung the tankard on the wall, and it is said that if it was ever moved or touched, loud noises would be heard on the beach, and ill luck would strike the Marsden Grotto.

On 5 December 2003, I joined Ghost Haunted North East in their investigation of the Grotto. Having read many articles in the press about activity, from visible 'orbs' to cold spots and electromagnetic fluctuations (not to mention the smuggler's screams!) it promised to be an interesting night. I was aware that the Allan tankard on display wasn't the original which had being 'spirited away' during one of the many periods the Grotto lay empty… so that added another dimension to the night.

By the time the investigation got underway (rather late after the last customer left) Ghost Haunted's medium had picked up activity on the pebble beach outside the Grotto, saying he could see that bodies had once washed up on the shore, victims of some sort of sacrifice. He also pointed to a small cave north of the Grotto, saying that it would be worthwhile to check it out.

Just after midnight we went outside with the medium, and again he mentioned bodies on the shore which might have been smugglers. He said he could see a small boy and a woman who had something to do with a dance hall (where the main Grotto bar area is now has been a dance hall in the past). He also picked up on the name Charles, and said that there were a confusing number of spirits shouting at him from the beach. We took photographs, but with the weather conditions so cold and windy and a lot of sea spray in the air, any anomalies caught on camera were probably just products of the environment. It was impossible to take temperature readings for the same reason.

On the way back to the Grotto some members of the team saw a flash of light on the wall of the patio, just as the medium said the spirit of a lady had walked through: however, I guessed the light was a reflection from the metal clip on

my clipboard. It is interesting, however, that the effect could not be duplicated.

Inside the Grotto, the medium picked up on a woman who liked to move or touch things in the kitchen, possibly one of the building's old cooks or servants. He also said that there was a presence in the ladies' toilets. Towards the kitchens he picked up on the term 'blaster', saying there was a man named Jack daring someone to go into the main Grotto alone later in the night, where he would do something to show he was there. Naturally, I volunteered!

The group split into teams at 2am and went their separate ways. The team members who headed along the beach towards the little cave certainly felt the brunt of the North Sea in November with lashing winds and salt air, and got very little of note from the area. Even with night-vision cameras, the lighting was poor. It has to be said that when you need a wake-up at 3am, two minutes standing on the North East coast will certainly do the trick!

The second floor restaurant proved more hospitable and well illuminated by the emergency lights. We got strong results from pendulum dowsing, indicating the presence of children, and, of even more interest, a digital dictaphone was set running to see if any EVP could be captured – each time the pendulum dowsing indicated a 'yes' there is a definite tap on the microphone. The team medium later confirmed that there were children present in that area.

Downstairs in one of the alcoves near the kitchen, the

team got some interesting results, all caught on camcorder. One of the team members attempted to communicate using dowsing rods; the one in his level and steady right hand started spinning faster and faster. Interesting as this is, it became more so when he asked the rod to stop – and it did, rather too suddenly!

In the bar area, the team medium saw a partially formed apparition on the cave side, as did one of the other investigators. Motion sensors were set to try and capture it again, but sadly got nothing. As for my solo stint in the cave as a result of 'Jack's' challenge, surrounded by night vision cameras, candles, with coin and dice trigger objects set, there was nothing doing except perhaps a very slight temperature drop (though that could be put down to the air vent in the ceiling above) and some strange shadow movement on the walls.

Other sensitives in the group mentioned that on the night in question, there was a bigger concentration of 'energy' on the beach itself and out towards Marsden Rock: one person even felt that a choir was singing from the top of the rock itself – a historical fact without a doubt, but also one I feel might have been the result of suggestion, as the Grotto itself exhibits photographs and images of the choir on the rock.

As far as I am aware, when the various Ghost Haunted members with camcorders reviewed their footage, they found nothing of interest, though one said that sitting in rooms murmuring, 'haway man we naa that ya in here wif wa, will ya dee somethin forra' might not have been the best way to provoke a response!

The Grotto's comfortable feeling is mixed with a strange combination of long shadows and deep dark corners. Ghost Haunted's medium picked up many names on the night, some of which have proved historically accurate, but many of which are impossible to trace as smugglers generally didn't leave a paper trail. Sceptics will say that many of the names, especially Jack the Blaster, are well known, as the legends surrounding the Grotto are centuries rather than decades old. The lack of hard physical data such as temperature anomalies was disappointing, though the footage showing the spinning dowsing rods that stopped suddenly when asked to was very interesting indeed. The strange tapping on the digital dictaphone in the restaurant area is also rather difficult to explain, as it was in plain view of the team at all times and not touched in any way. Nevertheless, visitors to the Grotto can rest assured that while enjoying a scrumptious meal or friendly drink overlooking Marsden Bay, they may not be the only ones there!

The ballroom at Marsden Grotto around 1890.

22. Welcome to Wonderland

Case Studies 9 April and 11 June 2004
Ravensworth Castle, Gateshead

Ravensworth Castle has been called called 'one of the lost treasures of Tyneside', few people knowing of its existence never mind its full and rich history. The Castle lies in the heart of the (very) private Ravensworth Estate in Tyne and Wear, and consists mostly of the remains of a medieval castle mingled with the ruins of an 18th-19th century building, surrounded by lush woodland and farmland. The earliest remains have been dated to the late 13th century, with two towers and some walling still in place. The rest of the ruined structure consists of a large house, built by the Liddell family in 1724, and the remains of a 19th-century Gothic castle, begun in 1808 by the renowned architect John Nash and finished after his death in 1846. Of this, the most substantial structure is the Nash Tower, and beneath that the dark and intact Nash cellars. Sadly, the castle was demolished in the 1950s.

The first known record of Ravensworth is 'Ravenshelm', mentioned in the 12th century by Symeon of Durham, as belonging to Bishop Flambard. Flambard left the estate to his nephew Richard, and it remained in the family until the 14th century when it passed to the Lumleys. In the second half of the 15th century, Ravensworth went to the Gascoignes, and in turn they sold it to Thomas Liddell, a prosperous merchant, in 1607. In 1642, Thomas Liddell (Sheriff of Newcastle) helped defend Newcastle against the Scots and received a baronetcy as his reward. Two hundred years later Sir Thomas Henry Liddell was made Lord Ravensworth, and he commis-

The Liddell house and main gate from the outside road.

sioned Nash to build the castle. He was also a leading light in the coal industry which ironically caused the destruction of the castle. It was built over a 30-acre coalfield, which had been heavily mined, and in 1953 the castle was demolished because of subsidence.

Henry George Liddell was another Ravensworth Liddell of note who moved to Cambridge and became the Dean of Christchurch College. He was a close friend of Lewis Carroll, and it is said that Henry's daughter, Alice Liddell, and the Ravensworth Estate itself, inspired Carroll's *Alice in Wonderland*.

During the 1920s, after the estate had begun to decline because of death duties, the Liddells moved their family seat from Ravensworth to Eslington Park in Northumberland.

The castle became a girl's boarding school until it was closed in 1932, when the first signs of subsidence were reported. In the 1950s one of the grandest castles in the North East was lost and 50 years later very few even knew of its existence. In 2003 the castle was featured on BBC2's *Restoration* programme.

It was a privilege for the Otherworld North East team to investigate the ruins of Ravensworth Castle, especially for me, as I had the added interest of exploring a little Liddell family history.

The team arrived at Ravensworth on 9th April 2004 at 10pm to meet the Head Gamekeeper, Barry, who showed us around the grounds, drawing particular attention to ruined floors and ceilings. One of the grounds staff declared: 'You'll not find anything in here…' a phrase which will probably go down in the annals of Otherworld North East!

Ravensworth Castle from the Liddell house.

At 11pm, Ghost Haunted North East's medium, who was with the team for the night, arrived and immediately said he had picked up on residual energy in the grounds. He walked around, recorded by dictaphone and, when the weather allowed, camcorder.

After ten minutes he asked where the portcullis was (none of the current arches have portcullis slots) and Barry confirmed that a temporary gatehouse with portcullis had indeed been built, but it had long since been pulled down. In the courtyard, the medium accurately identified the site of the stables and said that there was a man with the name of Nash there who'd used those stables to house his favourite horse.

Next to the ruined clock tower, the medium picked up on a group of girls, but said he could make no sense of it. He started to cough and said that at some point there had been a fire in that area; again the gamekeeper was able to confirm this. The medium asked if there was a source of water with a mining and railroad connection nearby, and noted a Henry Liddell with a strong connection to coal.

Interestingly, as soon as the group moved into one of the towers the medium picked up on a name that he didn't know how to spell, and said that it belonged to a man from either the seventh or eighth century. After questioning, the medium said the name was Hjuare, and was possibly Scandinavian. It has to be said that although no evidence is known to exist for settlement in that period Ravensworth, the presence of both Roman and medieval artefacts and structures found in the vicinity does make it likely.

Back in the courtyard, the medium picked up on Henry Liddell again with the name Thomas for the same man. The medium told me that Henry (or Thomas) was standing in

Two mists caught on 35mm camera between the two medieval towers. There was no visible mist at all that night!

front of me so I photographed the spot with a 35mm camera. The resulting two photographs show a thick mist that was certainly invisible at the time! More strangely, the frame taken between the two mist photographs shows no mist at all, indicating that it wasn't just moisture on the lens.

The medium said that he was picking up on a man watching the group from a distance, from the surrounding forest. As soon as one of the investigators approached the spot, the man vanished. The medium heard the name 'Charles Worthing' but he said he didn't think it belonged to the man he'd just seen.

With the initial walk around completed, the team split up for separate vigils.

The cellars under the ruins of the Nash Tower proved immediately interesting. At 12.48am, my group headed into the dark depths (an eerie looking place) and the medium was drawn to one of the rooms, where his temperature began to fluctuate wildly from 5.5°C to 22°C, one of the greatest differences I have ever seen. At this point the night vision cameras started to pick up speeding light anomalies around the medium, and luckily I caught two on digital camera. The medium said there was a frail dark-haired young woman in her mid-20s present who could hear our voices but couldn't see us. He got the date 1564 for her death, and that she'd died from tuberculosis: at this point he was shuddering and his temperature was at 6°C.

His skin temperature dropping to 5.5°C, he claimed to have picked up on an Abby or Abigail who was crying, having been beaten and 'abused' by her master in life. The medium's temperature was now rising and falling between 5.5 and 10°C and the rest of the team were feeling uncomfortable in the rapidly chilling atmosphere. The medium reported that

Even on a bright day the cellar entrance looks dark and forbidding. Since the investigations the cellar has been sealed …

Abby's abuser and his friends had knocked her teeth out, and that she had been blackmailed with threats of being accused of witchcraft. After the atmosphere lifted and the medium confirmed that the spirit was gone. His temperature rose to 22°C and remained steady.

Once we had composed ourselves, we followed the medium into an adjoining area of the cellars, where I and another

Mist caught on digital camera in the cellars. It was accompanied by untraceable sounds of muffled footsteps.

Danny felt as though something was behind him as this photograph was taken. No mist was visible to the naked eye.

team member heard crunching sounds of movement in the corridor behind us. I found the medium standing still by a wall and his temperature plummeted again from 22°C to 6°C. He seemed to be going into a trance, and three of us witnessed his features apparently beginning to change. In trance, he told me to 'get out!' but being stubborn (or perhaps stupid) I decided not to … The medium came out of his trance, his temperature rose steadily back to 22°C and he said all he could remember was a male presence but couldn't get a name.

At that point, one of the gamekeepers with the group felt a sharp prod in his back. He turned around to see who it was but found no-one there. Unnerved, he asked to take a break,

so two coins were set up in a sealed box as trigger objects and the investigators headed out of the cellars at 1.30am. We felt we were being followed and heard the unmistakeable sound of movement in the rooms around us.

Twenty minutes later the second group of investigators headed into the cellar, but reported it to be quite 'quiet'. Two of the team saw a dark shadow move away from them, and a distinct bright 'orb' was detected on night-vision camera. The investigator with the camera also felt a cold spot in one of the corridors, and many of the team heard a tapping noise that was later identified simply as dripping water.

As dawn broke at 4.50am, I headed back into the cellars with some of the team, to be greeted by the sound of shuffling footsteps and an atmosphere so charged that you could almost feel your hair standing on end (incidentally, EMF surveys showed *no* results).

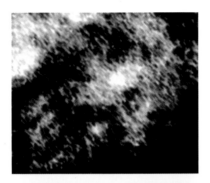

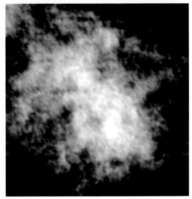

Computer enhancements of two 'faces' in the mist in the picture of Danny, opposite.

Five minutes later we settled in one of the rooms, and I started the photographic survey. At one point the temperature dropped noticeably and a second shot of the same area shows a mist rolling off the ceiling, though nothing was visible to the naked eye.

One of the investigators asked for 'anyone' present to show a sign, whereupon he suddenly seemed to develop a problem speaking and I saw what for all the world looked

'If there's anything there please show yourself.'

like finger impressions on his throat! The investigator's skin temperature dropped from 16°C to 4°C, and quite suddenly we all heard what sounded like footsteps in the corridors. I also identified the sound of swishing cloth and the temperature bounced between 10 and 18°C. The investigator who seemed to be being choked felt his torch hit by something; the rest of us heard the impact clearly.

At 5.07am, one of the group – possibly rashly – asked for more signs. One team member felt something 'blowing' on his ear. I noticed a flash of light over his shoulder, but another investigator described it as a face. A photograph taken at the time shows a thick mist rolling over him from behind, although nothing was visible. Some people looking at the photograph claim to see a face in the mist, but I would be cautious as the human brain is programmed to pick out faces in random images.

Three minutes later two of us saw movement in the corridor, but a sweep with torches showed nothing there. However, we could all hear shuffling sounds and what sounded like swishing skirts. We asked 'it' to show itself and a mist with a thick, almost solid edge appeared on the photographs.

Before we headed out into the rapidly brightening dawn light, the trigger object coins were checked; one had moved 1mm – not a lot, but still significant.

Though the cellars were perhaps the 'highlight' of the expedition, they were by no means the only area of Ravensworth where activity was recorded. In the southernmost 'Norman' tower of the castle, at 2.30am, the medium (whose temperature was fluctuating between 9.5 and 13.5°C) picked up on a male presence called Matthew, an apprentice blacksmith. Two members of the group reported hearing the sound of 'breathing' (which didn't come from any of the team members!) and when I tried pendulum dowsing there was a distinct static discharge up the pendulum chain. I set a digital dictaphone recording and picked up a long sigh, also heard by two other investigators.

At 2.40am, the crystal dowsing pendulum was pulled to an impossible angle, defying gravity, which was witnessed by several team members. A minute later something brushed past one of the ground staff – the air turned blue with choice (and very human) language as he expressed his shock! All anomalous readings vanished, so the team moved up one

level in the tower. Again the medium picked up Matthew, plus a Catherine or 'Kate', wearing a flowing red dress (a colourful change from all the Grey Ladies around the region). The medium's temperature was fluctuating, even though everyone else's in the room remained constant.

In the ruined clocktower one of the investigators, using dowsing rods, reported an almost childlike playful presence and in the northernmost 'Norman' tower the medium picked up the name of 'Gascoigne'. There was simply the feeling of being watched and followed through the entire night.

With what seemed like real hard evidence of paranormal activity at Ravensworth Castle, the team was delighted when the owner allowed a follow-up investigation to take place on 11th June. Few of us would forget it in a hurry!

In the time between the two investigations, staff on the estate had experienced more strange occurrences, which we needed to check out, investigating the old ponds and some of the old roads and pathways, as well as the castle and the cellars (which were still frighteningly active).

The path down to the south lodge of the estate proved fruitful for pendulum dowsing. Two dowsers picked up an 18 year-old male who had worked at the estate, his job involving music. Pipes and drums were mentioned; there were military tattoos held here in the 1930s. Near the castle, the team stopped at a crossroads and again tried dowsing, this time with two dowsers standing back to back, asking the same questions but not speaking the answer aloud. Seven questions were asked and the dowsers produced identical answers for six of them. They indicated a 13 year old boy who had worked on the estate. We would have asked more questions, but one of the dowsers started to feel very ill, describing the symptoms of pneumonia far too accurately for comfort!

Luckily, he felt better as soon as the group left the crossroads.

At the overgrown ponds, the investigators had a strong feeling of being watched. Staff said they had felt similar sensations in the very same place. A mild case of Blair Witch?

After EMF and photo sweeps of the area, entered a small caravan near the far pond. Dowsing picked up three separate entities. At 1am we identified a male who seemed to dislike gamekeepers and claimed to be part of the landowner's family, though the timeframe was never established. At the same time there was a power drain in our equipment. Half an hour later, a female made contact. She had been killed by her husband when he found her with another man. We all simultaneously experienced chronic back pain – then discovered the woman's fatal injury was back-related. During dowsing one of the team's surface body temperature fluctuated by 4°C.

An hour later, the next team picked up a male spirit in the caravan. Staff members said it sounded like the old Head Gamekeeper. There were sounds of movement outside and one of the team saw a dark shadow in the shape of a man. When he investigated he heard footsteps and a loud sigh, though no-one else was present.

In the courtyard and the Liddell house, there were no EMF anomalies, though the team had a real problem with battery drainage in both cameras and torches. Several investigators complained of nausea, headaches and sharp pains in their necks and shoulders through the course of the night. There was also a strong breeze which made dowsing difficult, but proved interesting when one investigator asked any spirit present to stop the pendulum blowing about. The response was immediate and strong; the pendulum stopped and held absolutely still even in the face of the wind. In the shelter of the main gateway, the dowsers picked up on a male presence,

The northern-most medieval tower, said to contain the spirits of Matthew and Catherine.

and the name Liddell, but nothing else. There was also the feeling of being watched from the one of ground floor rooms, and at 1.10am, two of the investigators saw a shadow move through that room and out through an old doorway, as if something had just 'passed through'. A lot of noises were heard, but these were probably a combination of the wind rattling through the ruin and local wildlife.

At 1.15am, two of the investigators, looking out of the window towards the Liddell house, saw a figure standing in the archway. They watched it for several minutes, though another investigator couldn't see anything. Three different cameras wouldn't focus on the area in question, so no photographs could be taken, much to our annoyance.

The cellars beneath the Nash tower gave the greatest

amount of evidence for paranormal activity. Over the course of the night four investigators undertook solo vigils in the dark depths, armed only with a walkie-talkie, a nightvision camcorder and a torch. The first vigil took place at 10.15pm, where, mid-way through the half hour, the investigator was startled by the sound of a beer can (one of the many left lying around by trespassing kids) being slowly crushed in the room where he was sitting. Luckily, the sound, and the investigator's reaction, were caught very nicely on camcorder!

At 1am things really started to hot up. The group in the cellars had split into two teams, in different rooms. One group challenged any spirits present to show themselves, hoping for similar results to those we had April, whilst the other group tried pendulum dowsing. At 1.05am, the first group heard a loud unidentified noise, which they described as a 'swooshing' sound. Seconds later, the other group saw a bright orange light approach. Quite suddenly one of the team was hit hard and knocked backwards, and the dowser was hurled into the cellar wall, the impact injuring her wrist. Understandably, chaos erupted, bringing a very rapid halt to the vigil.

At 1.30am, a very brave (or reckless) investigator went into the cellars for the third solo vigil of the night. The experiences of the previous team had been carefully explained to him, but he decided to do it anyway! Unfortunately, his camcorder died after only 10 minutes of use. Naturally previous events played on his imagination. He reported a number of strange sounds and sensations, but luckily he wasn't attacked!

An hour later, the new team in the cellars found that the wind chimes set as trigger objects were moving, without draught or wind, but neither the EMF or temperature survey picked up any anomalies. Dowsing was attempted, but the only response was very weak.

At 3.15am, I undertook the final solo investigation in the cellar, starting with a photographic, EMF and temperature survey which revealed nothing of interest. I filmed the room with the camcorder, while asking questions of anything present. For the first 20 minutes the room felt warm and comfortable, pitch dark and absolutely silent, and then quite suddenly the temperature dropped by 10°C in just under two seconds. I did another photo survey which revealed a mist behind me. Quickly I took another photograph but the mist had vanished – at that point the temperature went back to normal.

The dowsing in the last investigation in the cellar was relatively uneventful, with long periods of no responses, though at 4.23am each team member's surface body temperature started fluctuating by 8°C, and dowsing revealed the weak presence of a woman, who spelt her name 'Abigail', the name we'd picked up in the cellars on our previous visit.

The investigations at Ravensworth Castle were two of the most active I have taken part in with unquestionably 'anomalous' activity ranging from temperature fluctuations to noises and excellent photographic evidence, not to mention the undoubted impact that the attack in the cellars had on those involved. Many thanks must go to the owner of the estate, and to all the estate staff who have helped so enthusiastically during the investigations.

Ravensworth Castle – the glory days, around 1910.

23. LIGHTING THE WAY

Souter Lighthouse, South Shields

When Souter Lighthouse opened in 1871 it was considered very high-tech because it used alternating electric current. Today the lighthouse is a National Trust property with the engine room, light tower and keeper's living quarters all open to the public.

Of course, the lighthouse has at least one ghost. Living TV's *Most Haunted* investigated the site, as did one local paranormal investigation group.

The rather noisy ghost of Souter Lighthouse is said to be a colliery worker (from the nearby Marsden colliery) who lived at the complex in the 1920s – the flat area of grass to the north of the Lighthouse is the site of the old colliery village. The ghost bangs doors, particularly in the tea-rooms. Staff have found items moved and heard the unmistakable sounds of footsteps walking the empty corridors. There is often a strong smell of tobacco and the ghost seems to be more active during periods of disruption like decorating, renovations or other building work.

Investigators on 18 November 2002, heard about a 'ghostly lighthouse keeper' from the owner of the lighthouse, as well as the spirit of a young woman named Isabella who was said to walk the complex. The team spent an uneasy night looking for traces of Souter's ghostly inhabitants, recording a loud crash heard from the corner of the Engine Room at 12.45am, accompanied by heavy static interference that resembled a 'fluttering noise' on the team's walkie-talkies. At 2.45am two investigators heard footsteps walking down one of the corridors, but on checking the area thoroughly, found no one there.

Souter Lighthouse, 1928, the remains of the old mining village in the foreground.

24. MONK'S HOOD

Tynemouth Priory and Castle

Tynemouth Priory and Castle are one of the North East's treasures, with a long history to match their impressive and imposing presence on the headland overlooking the north side of the mouth of the Tyne. There has been a fortification on the site since at least the Norman invasion, and the Priory has a history of royal burials including the King of Deira and Malcolm II of Scotland, though the Scottish King's remains were moved to Dunfermline Abbey at a later date.

If the ghostly tales surrounding the Castle and Priory are to be believed, the history of the area stretches back at least to the time of the Viking invasions, when legend has it, a wounded marauder named Olaf was taken in by the monks of Tynemouth and nursed back to health, where he became a brother of the order. Soon afterwards the Vikings raided the coast again, the marauding party this time including Olaf's brother who was killed in the conflict. Olaf is said to have collapsed and died from grief in the chapel while praying for his brother's soul. Since then the ghostly figure of Olaf, it is said, can be seen looking out to sea on stormy nights, contemplating the death of his brother.

The picture dates from around 1890 when the Castle was used as a barracks.

25. Tales of the Tyneside

Case Study 31 October 2003

Tyneside Cinema, Newcastle upon Tyne

The Tyneside Cinema on Pilgrim Street is near the sites of the Newe House, General Leven's headquarters during the Civil War, and Greyfriars Monastery (founded 1237).

The building opened its doors on 1st February 1937 as a News Theatre, a relatively new innovation aimed at people with an hour or two to spare. Designed by Mr. George Bell, built by Thomas Clements and owned by Dixon Scott, it seated 252 people in the stalls and 160 in the balcony.

Programmes lasted seventy-five minutes and included news reels, cartoons, sport and travel films. The building also had coffee rooms and a private cinema. By the 1950s, however, news theatres were struggling to compete with television news; its two Newcastle competitors went out of business in 1959. The News Theatre survived until March 1968, when the building was taken over by the Tyneside Film Theatre and subsequently the Tyneside Cinema.

On Friday 31 October 2003, I joined the Ghost Haunted North East team, a student documentary film crew and a BBC reporter for an overnight investigation. Because it was Hallowe'en, we were expecting a very active night.

We set up motion sensors in corridors, lock-off video cameras and trigger objects to check for any curious ghosts.

At once the medium began picking up names associated with the property: specifically a Thomas Clarence or Clemence, two men by the names of Dixon Scott and Dixon Scott Junior, and the words 'I built this.' On the top floor he also said that he could see the Pathé News logo on the screen and got the impression that the building had initially been rejected as a cinema.

In the second floor corridor leading to the main office, the medium said that sometimes people walking there would feel shoved or prodded. The air temperature was fluctuating between 26° and 28.6°C, and there was a strange feeling of being watched but no EMF readings except those caused by nearby power sockets and cables.

Two of us felt a watching presence in the private cinema on the second floor, though a temperature survey and EMF sweep provided no results. However, a few digital photographs taken in this area during the course of the night show 'orbs'. These photos are dark and further analysis of them was inconclusive so perhaps the anomalies were just the result of dust being disturbed by the investigators.

At 12.30am, the medium picked up on the presence of a mischievous spirit in the main cinema; he started flipping the seats three times to demonstrate what this spirit sometimes did. Seat-flipping is said to occur, but not in that particular theatre!

The medium led the team into the projection room, following the spirit. There the picked up on a Edward Charles, or a Charles Edward who used to work at the Cinema. Through the medium, Charles said that the cinema had been built in 1937 as a News Theatre. The medium also picked up on the word 'Dutch' or 'Deutsch', Pathé news, the name of Oscar, and that the cinema possibly had Odeon connections. He told the team that the spirit in the projection room often frequented the women's toilets, and that he found the investigators fascinating. He said the spirit was confused when looking at the crew's cameras, as he'd never heard of 'Sony'!

At 1am in the second floor corridor, I tried, without success, to show the documentary crew how pendulum dowsing worked. However, as soon as the crew moved on, the pendulum responded, and indicated that the spirit in the corridor disliked crowds. During the brief period of communication the temperature fluctuated between 28.1°C and 30.3°C. When the medium returned with the group, he identified an area of the corridor as a 'vortex'. As he was pointing out

The second floor corridor.

the affected area the temperature began move rapidly from 24° to 30.4° to 28.4°C. The team followed the medium to the first floor corridor, where he picked up the same phenomenon, as if the activity in one corridor was directly related to that on the floor below.

Ten minutes we moved into the private cinema where the medium picked up on the name Kate Filbin, the ghost of a woman who would, he claimed, often be seen going into the adjoining restaurant-bar. At one point the temperature here jumped from 25°C to 29°C. Kate, he said, enjoyed the sugar lumps on the bar!

At 2.12am, we set up a digital dictaphone in the first

floor corridor in an attempt to record some EVP. We tried dowsing again, this time picking up a young man, aged 31, who had worked at the cinema. The dowser's temperature was moving from 24°C to 30°C. We left the corridor but sadly the EVP we had left running picked up no anomalous sounds after we had gone.

Throughout the night, light anomalies were picked up in the two 'active' corridors both on video and cam-

A computer enhanced photograph of a light anomaly on the balcony.

era, and moving anomalies were recorded on the lock-off video camera in the top floor projection room. However EVP tests failed to pick up anything out of the ordinary. Interestingly, the spiritual presences picked up by the medium had nothing to do with the medieval hooded figures reported by staff and customers at the Tyneside Cinema. Next time you go to see a film at the Tyneside and feel a slight chill in one of the corridors, smile and say hello in case an invisible presence is passing by.

26. THE UNFORTUNATE BOB

Tyne Theatre and Opera House

The Tyne Theatre and Opera House opened on 18 September 1867. The Opera House had a special effects sound system including an ingenious thunder roll device. However, this effect was the cause of a tragedy which was reported in the *Newcastle Courant* on 8 April 1887:

Last night, about nine o'clock, a serious accident occurred to a man named Robert Courtenedge, 30 yrs of age, millwright, at the Tyne Theatre, Newcastle. It appears whilst the avalanche scene was being carried out in the performance of the new opera 'Nordisa', a cannon-ball, a 36 pounder, was rolled along a surface to cause the effect of stage thunder. After the ball had rolled along the required distance it dropped into a box which was placed to receive it, but instead of remaining, it fell out, by some means as yet unknown, on to a rostrum and from there it dropped a distance of about twelve feet on to Courtenedge's head, fracturing his skull.

The unfortunate Robert Courtenedge didn't survive his encounter with the cannon ball, and it is said that his startled looking ghost, known to staff as 'Bob' haunts the

The elaborate Tyne Theatre saloon around 1895.

Newcastle Opera House to this day. The theatre's website reports that Bob appeared to stage staff on two successive Thursdays during the pantomime season of 2000.

27. CULTURE CLASH

Case Study 26 March and 30 May 2004
Washington Art Centre, Washington

Washington Art Centre in Fatfield was investigated twice during 2004, first on 26 March by Ghost Haunted North East then on 30 May by the north-east based paranormal research group TAPS (The Answers People Seek). I accompanied both teams.

The art centre is built on the site of a late medieval farm and some of the old buildings are incorporated in the structure. There are tales of a suicide in the room now used as the theatre which is haunted by a ghostly figure said to sit at the back of the auditorium. Spectres have been seen wandering up staircases and through walls, and there are noises and crashes so loud that in the early 1990s local residents made a formal complaint about the noise coming from the centre late one night, only to find the place was closed and empty. Staff have reported bottles thrown from shelves in the public bar, a strange scent of roses has been noted on numerous occasions, radios have changed channels unexpectedly and beer taps have been tampered with. In the mid 1980s a coin-operated polaroid camera was triggered during the night and recorded what looked like the misty face of a woman. Needless to say, the staff member who found the photograph the next morning was more than a little surprised!

At the beginning of the investigation on 26 March one of the team picked up on a child in the top floor function room. The impression was so strong that she started to hum 'Pop Goes the Weasel' which she said the child was singing, her body temperature was fluctuating by a massive 12°C.

In the low barn area the same team member reported she could see a young girl with blonde hair, dressed like an old fashioned stable worker. Though no electromagnetic anomalies were recorded, there was a spot 4°C colder than the rest of the room precisely where the spirit girl was standing.

In the centre of the room the group tried some pendulum dowsing, and though the responses were weak they indicated a male who had died there at the age of 29. This result was gained independently by two different people. Later on one

The old and new haunted buildings of Washington Arts Centre.

of the guests got a good strong result on her pendulum, picking up a young woman who indicated she was the one who left the scent of roses around the place.

At just after 1am, the group moved into the theatre to see if they could find a trace of the ghostly suicide victim said to haunt the stage and seats. Everyone reported a sense of unease, so we did an electromagnetic and temperature sweep. The investigators also tried pendulum dowsing, but stopped quickly when the pendulum started swinging in a near-perfect triangle, a movement which is rather improbable. The dowser felt she'd been approached from behind by a woman and said that the name 'Eva' had popped into her head.

When we moved to the upper bar at 3am the entire team could feel the chill in the air. In the kitchen, an electromagnetic and temperature sweep located a spot 5°C colder than the rest of the kitchen so two of us tried pendulum dowsing there. The results indicated a male called Michael who had worked for the Lambtons and been murdered. During the questioning, the dowser's temperature was bouncing between 23° and 30°C though there was no breeze. Contact with Michael faded soon after he revealed how he had died; his legs were broken then he was decapitated – certainly not a nice end, but it did make one investigator who had developed a painful neck earlier on wonder about its source!

The art centre's owner said the same results had been produced by a visiting medium in the kitchen years before.

By 4.30am we were getting tired. Two of us decided to try a silent vigil in the theatre, almost immediately hearing the unmistakeable sounds of someone walking towards us across the stage floor. No-one else was in the theatre. When we turned around from the stage, we both saw a flash of light across the wall but we couldn't trace its source.

A moving light anomaly was caught on nightvision camcorder by one of the investigation guests. It looks almost like a bubble of light floating down through the theatre before vanishing off-screen – an anomaly unlike anything we had witnessed before.

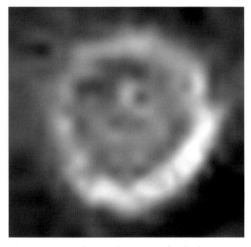

Computer enhanced image of a light anomaly photographed in the back bar.

The second investigation began with strong dowsing results in the lower back bar. The bar was warm and comfortable, but two members felt that one of the corners had a certain 'feel' to it – it was actually 3°C colder than the rest of the room. Dowsing indicated two spirits in the bar area; a young man and a young woman. The woman was dominant and almost 'chatty'. She had worked at the centre when it had been a farm and had died at the age of seventeen when she was kicked by a horse. She was unable to say when she lived. Interestingly, while some of the investigation guests were dowsing in the bar, a light 'orb' anomaly hovering around them, was caught on digital camera. Could this have been the spirit that was seen two months earlier in the low barn?

The rest of the night consisted of periods of uneventful silence followed by short bursts of extremely strange activity. In the lower barn, one group came across a bizarre electromagnetic anomaly: on the initial sweep of the area, no anomalies were found (other than the power generated by the electrics in the bar) but on a subsequent sweep there was a small anomaly which hadn't been there before by one of the tables. After a matter of seconds, the reading vanished again. Surprised by this, I asked anything present to move to the table again. Once again the EMF meter picked up an anomaly which swiftly vanished. Ten minutes later another investigator, who hadn't been present when we found this anomaly, thought he saw the dark shape of a man standing by the very same table, though nothing showed up on the night vision cameras.

To me the strangest part of the complex was the corridor running parallel to the theatre. Whether dark or fully lit, there was always the strong feeling of being watched, with perhaps the faintest of traces of an extra footfall or rustle of movement. Imagination or not, the medium who visited the Centre with TAPS did say that anyone heading to the toilets along that corridor would not be alone!

Reputedly, the most active area of Washington Arts Centre is the theatre.

28. Stars and Stripes

Case Study 14 May 2004
Washington Old Hall, Washington near Sunderland

Washington Old Hall, currently under the care of the National Trust, is not the first building to stand on the site. It is thought that in the 12th century, when the lands passed to William of Washington from the Bishop of Durham, there was probably no more than a tower or fortified house here. The hall was added around 100 years later. In 1613 the Washington estate once more passed into the hands of the Bishop of Durham and the house was restructured into a comfortable home. By then the Washington family had moved to Northamptonshire where they became successful wool merchants. One of their descendants was George Washington, first President of the United States.

Washington Old Hall fell on hard times. There were numerous tenants and by the 19th century it was home to over 30 people living in squalid conditions. The state of the hall was so bad that it was scheduled for demolition in 1936. However, a local preservation committee stepped in to save the building. It was restored to its

Jacobean condition and opened to the public in 1955.

It has been said that strange sounds can be heard in the hall at night, and that a grey lady haunts the corridors. Often the smell of lavender permeates some rooms.

On Friday 14th May 2004 I joined Dean Maynard and his team, plus members of the Blue Water Spiritual Healing Centre. We started at 10pm and the team split to cover the hall, working in hour long vigils.

As the investigations started we heard the creaks and groans that come from all old buildings as they settle in the

Washington Old Hall on the night of the investigation.

night-time chill. The rooms of the Hall were quite warm but there were small localised cold spits in many places, especially the first floor bedroom and the kitchen area off the Great Hall. Some were easily tracked to windows or doors, but in other cases there were no explanations with spots measuring 5°C colder than surrounding areas. Activity reported by the 'sensitives' in my group seemed to correlate with anomalies picked up by the instruments, whether it was digital temperature gun or photography. In the kitchen the temperature anomalies seemed to move around the room, and one of the mediums suggested that they were the spirits of children, as well as a cook. The medium felt something nip his arm and at that precise point his temperature dropped briefly by 4°C. Interestingly, the kitchen is also one of the places in the Hall which visitors, including members of the Otherworld North East team, have reported as being 'busy' with movement, even during the day.

In the Great Hall several team members heard, for an instant, the sound of metal clinking against metal. The medium told the group that he could see a man standing in one of the doorways, holding an old style keyring, laden with keys … interesting, as at that point no-one in the group had mentioned that they'd heard the metallic sound!

However, most activity was witnessed in the Panelled Room, just off the Great Hall. In a previous investigation the GHNE crew had observed numerous 'orbs' flying around the Panelled Room on a lock-off camera and we were hoping to record something on our instruments. The group held a séance in the panelled room, resulting in loud bangs and crunches from the wall and temperature drops. Most amazingly, everyone saw the vase in the middle of the table move an inch or two. Afterwards, the room had a cold feeling and was 4°C colder than it had been before the séance.

Immediately after, another group held a séance in the room which I observed and photographed. The noises heard during the séance could well have been taps and bangs coming from the back wall – or could have been simply the building still settling. Perhaps our own weight on the floorboards was making the walls shift minutely. However, under ultra-violet light I did see a very faint mist behind two investigators – both of whom later reported feeling chilled. Much to my annoyance the mist didn't show up on my photographs. The sound recording didn't pick up anything unusual either, though at the time when I saw the mist there does seem to be very minor interference on the recording that sounds as though something was muffling the voices in the room.

So does Washington Old Hall deserve the title of being a haunted building? There is lots of evidence in the form of light and temperature anomalies and information provided by the sensitives. The movement of the vase during the séance also seems to be a very strong indication that there is a presence there.

29. A 19th Century Investigation

Willington Millhouse, Willington Quay

The story of a very early paranormal investigation is related by Eric Forster in his book *Weird Tales of Northumbria*. In 1840 two men decided to search for the ghost of Willington Mill and to put it to rest. They got permission from the flour mill's owner, Joseph Proctor, a Quaker, who had moved there in 1829. According to local legend, the adjoining mansion, in which the Proctor family lived, was built on the site of an old house which had suffered from nearly two centuries of hauntings. In 1800, when the mansion was built, the ghosts tried harder to make their presence known, with strange sounds of banging, dragging and the occasional moan. With regard to the hauntings, William Richardson says in his History of Wallsend that 'evidence by absolutely sane, unimpeachable witnesses … is overwhelming'.

Four trustworthy witnesses had seen a bare-headed man, dressed in robes, appear at an upper window and perform 'various rituals' before vanishing. The spectral sounds of footsteps were also heard at night, accompanied by heavy knocking on doors – though no intruder was ever found on the premises.

On another occasion, two sisters visiting the house claimed that during the night their bed had floated up off the floor. On their second night in the room they were even more terrified by the bed being shaken and the bed curtains opening and closing rapidly. Hoping to rid themselves of their mischievous visitor, the women asked for the curtains to be taken down. To their utter terror they saw a full apparition of a woman, glowing slightly with a pale blue light, gliding across the bed and through the headboard. After this incident, the two women would never set foot in that room again, and had to be housed elsewhere!

And so, in the summer of 1840, Mr Hudson and Mr Drury (armed with some pistols, just in case!) arrived at the millhouse. They considered the hauntings to be the product of hysteria and imagination. They began their vigil on the upper floor stairhead. Lighting two wax candles they settled down to observe.

Two hours passed without anything happening. Then, at a quarter past midnight, a strange 'hollow sound' echoed through the house. Things seemed to quiet again, and then there were more sounds, like wagon wheels rumbling over cobbles. When they heard the sound of bare feet in a bedroom to Hudson's right they remembered that they'd left their pistols downstairs, well out of reach.

However, as often happens, the sounds suddenly ceased and both men became drowsy.

Forster reproduces Dr. Drury's account of what happened next:

… I took up a note which I had accidentally dropped and began to read it; after which I took out my watch to ascertain the time … In taking my eyes from the watch they became riveted upon a closet door which I distinctly saw open, and also saw the figure of a female, attired in greyish garments, with the head inclined downwards, and one hand pressed upon the chest as if in pain, and the other – the right hand – extended towards the floor, with the index finger pointing downwards … It advanced with an apparently cautious step across the floor towards me … Immediately as it approached my friend, who was

*slumbering, its right hand extended towards him. I then
rushed at it, giving at the time ... a most awful yell but,
instead of grasping it, I fell upon my friend.*

Drury's yell woke the household (as well as Hudson!) and
they had to carry the doctor downstairs in an 'agony of fear
and terror'. However, Hudson saw nothing. He investigated
all the rooms around the stairhead but found nothing unusual.

By the end of the 19th century, the male ghost on the top
floors had been seen so many times that he'd been given the
nickname 'Old Jeffrey'. The woman in grey was often seen
around the house, sometimes wrapped in a mantle. Anyone
who saw her face realised that she had no eyes. One of the
other ghostly manifestations was said to be that of a child,
with light running footsteps and a horrible chilling laugh ...

DURHAM & TEESSIDE

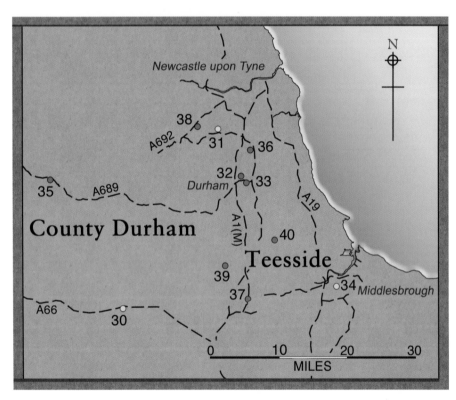

30. Emma's Room

Case Study 23 July 2004
The Ancient Unicorn Inn, Bowes

The Ancient Unicorn Inn is on the main street of Bowes on the southern edge of County Durham. Several famous travellers have stayed there, including Charles Dickens who was researching *Nicholas Nickelby*. The inn is reputed to be haunted by at least three ghosts. A bearded fellow in a bowler hat has been seen wandering around the premises. A young man with dark hair is often seen by the fireplace. The most active and well known of the Unicorn's resident ghosts is a young girl known as Emma, who is seen all around the building as a full apparition. Visitors have reported hearing a party going on downstairs when there was no-one there, and spotted Emma wearing a green party dress.

The tale goes that Emma fell in love with a young man but her father didn't approve, so they used to meet in secret, often on the moors. One night there was a violent storm and her beloved died of exposure. Emma soon followed him to the grave with a broken heart. Since that day, the spirit of Emma is said to haunt the Ancient Unicorn, and the young dark haired man is thought to be the ghost of her beloved.

On 23 July 2204, the Otherworld North East team arrived at the inn. Even before the investigation started at 1am one of the team saw a shadowy figure in the doorway leading from the bar to the car park. When he concentrated on it the figure vanished. The same investigator saw the figure again in the doorway at 2.16am, and again the shape vanished when he looked closely at it. Unfortunately photographs showed nothing at all. Four minutes later, another

member of the team, now alone in the bar, had a fleeting glimpse of a young man with long dark hair standing at the bar, but no EMF or temperature fluctuations were discovered. At 2.20am, the jar of sweets on the bar started to rattle, stopped suddenly, and started again ten minutes later. We could find no reason for this. At 3.05am, the investigator who had twice seen the shadowy figure saw it again in the bar. This time he tried not to look directly at it, and got the impression that it was a female. The figure vanished when we tried to photograph it.

At 2.20am, one investigator set up camp at the base of the inn's main stairwell as the landlady had seen the apparition of Emma there. He set a night vision camcorder and a digital dictaphone. EMF and temperature surveys gave no results, and it was over half an hour before there was any activity. At 2.55am he felt something tugging at his utility belt and heard a tapping noise with no apparent source. The tugging lasted for about 15 seconds. Three minutes later he thought he could hear female voices, raised slightly in anger, and then a clear voice pronounced the letters 'M', 'N' and 'E'.

There was activity in the restaurant almost as soon as the first vigil began at 1am. A camcorder was set running in nightshot mode, and a brass key was used as a trigger object. The investigators' torch started to drain quickly, but an EMF survey gave no results. The ambient air temperature was 18°C. When the survey was completed the torch seemed to right itself.

The team tried pendulum dowsing under ultra-violet light. Although reactions were very weak they indicated the presence of a 17-year-old female. At 1.14am a loud bang was heard from the doorway to the kitchen, and then the dowser's surface body temperature started to fluctuate between 25-28°C, at the same time as the ultra-violet light's batteries began to drain rapidly. The pendulum seemed to be pulled strongly in random directions, and then the observing team member felt something touch his left cheek. A minute later, he heard shuffling footsteps behind the team, and his own temperature began to fluctuate between 25-27°C. One photograph shows an elongated bright orange and red light anomaly over one of the tables, but it was merely a refraction (how easy it is to produce anomalies which prove perfectly natural!). The next session of dowsing produced stronger results and indicated the presence of a young woman and her father, who seemed to be a restraining influence. When the woman was asked her name, the pendulum spelt 'I A M E M' before

The anomaly that never was … this red light caught on digital camera in the restaurant was just a refraction from a mirror.

coming to an abrupt halt. At the same time there were two loud thumping noises in the room. It is tempting to interpret the letters as 'I am Em...'

At 2.15am, another investigator in the restaurant reported feeling as though something was pressing fingers into her shoulder, but neither EMF nor temperature anomalies were found. At 2.30am, the team had camera trouble in the room, with batteries being drained as quickly as they were loaded. Once again shuffling noises were heard coming from beside the kitchen door. As soon as the team tried to record this, the camera drained of all power and the team's torch switched itself off!

At 2.50am, another dowser set to work in the restaurant, unaware of the results of the previous dowsing session. Again, the dowsing indicated a young female, who claimed to move around in the Dickens Room upstairs. When asked to spell her name, the pendulum identified her as an Emie Worthington, and said that the landlady referred to her as

Emma. At 3.30am, there was a loud bang from the kitchen, and an investigator saw a shadowy figure in the kitchen doorway. It vanished rapidly, then there was a bizarre set of clicking sounds which couldn't be tracked to their source.

Upstairs in the Dickens Room, the vigil started quietly at 12.58am, with trigger objects set and EMF and temperature surveys picking up nothing. Then, at 1am, an 'orb' light anomaly passed over the arm of one of the investigators, so the team tried pendulum dowsing. The dowser picked up on a female, possibly over the age of 15. Suddenly the dowser cried out; she couldn't explain why but her body surface temperature had dropped by 3°C during dowsing. At 1.17am, the observer's camera refused to focus for 30 seconds, and then at 1.26am the dowser suddenly felt cold down her left side as if something had moved close. When checked, her right leg measured 34°C and, sure enough, her left leg only 29°C. At 1.30am she thought she could hear faint music coming from outside the room; four minutes later the floorboards creaked outside as if someone was walking along the corridor. The corridor was checked, but no-one could be found. The team tried to set a voice recorder, but the new batteries were drained dry within five seconds of starting the recording.

In 'Emma's Room', there were no EMF or temperature fluctuations at 2.40am. At 2.46am the team reported that something made the closed door creak as if it was being pushed from outside. The sound was closely followed by what they described as a 'clap' from the corridor. The dowser reported the presence of a female who said that she'd lived in the inn, and was bothered by another spirit. This female seemed unwilling to communicate and asked for the dowsing to stop, so the team had a break for ten minutes. When dowsing started again the girl spelt her name 'Em' and claimed

that she had been afraid of the first dowser. At 5.27am a loud thud was heard on the ceiling from the floor above: there was no-one up there at the time.

In the Pennine Room, the EMF sweep picked up no anomalies barring power cabling in the walls, and temperatures remained steady. At 1.06am dowsing picked up on a female spirit, 42 years old, who had visited the Inn in 1663 and had died there. The spirit spelt out her name as Barbara, but then communication stopped. No further activity was recorded until 4.13am when one of the investigators felt there was someone sitting on the next bed, and the camera refused to focus despite the strong light level in the room.

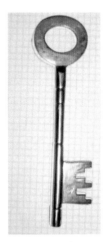

A trigger object, with an outline drawn around it to check for movement.

Finally, the cellars were investigated. At 3.35am the door swung half open and the key vibrated and rattled hard in the lock. Taking this as an invitation, the team moved down into the cellars and tried dowsing. There was a distinct chill in the air but this is not unusual in cellars! Dowsing indicated a male spirit, 'Paul' who was 15 years old when he died of consumption in 1604. Paul had worked at the Inn, was happy where he was, and often made small noises heard by the staff.

The investigation at the Ancient Unicorn was a little frustrating because it felt as if whatever haunts the Unicorn was keeping out of the way. Nevertheless, we identified four spirits; Barbara, Em and her father, and Paul, the boy in the cellar who was something of a surprise as the staff had not reported hearing or seeing anything down there.

31. A Stately Home

Case Studies 12 March and 7 May 2004
Beamish Hall, Beamish, Stanley

Though the County Durham village of Beamish (from the French *Bew mys* meaning 'beautiful mansion') is famous nationwide for its Open Air Museum, Beamish Hall, close to the museum, is relatively unknown. In 1268 (or 1309 depending on which source you use!) Philip de la Leigh gave his daughter and her new husband, Sir Bertram Monboucher, the Manor of Tanfield as a wedding gift. It is possible he also built the first hall at Beamish. The oldest part of the present building dates from 1620. In 1884 the Shafto family took possession through marriage. Most north-easterners know the song Bobby Shafto:

> *Bobby Shafto's gone to sea, silver buckles on his knee,*
> *He'll come back and marry me, Bonny Bobby Shafto.*

Few know however that Bobby Shafto not only left Beamish Hall but also deserted his fiancée when he went to sea, and this may be the cause of strange occurrences there.

While the Shaftos lived at the hall, Beamish was an active area in coalmining, ironworking and flint milling for Sunderland Ware pottery. The hall was extended between 1890 and 1909, and was probably used as a command centre during the World Wars. In 1952, death duties forced the Shafto family to sell Beamish Hall. It was used by the National Coal Board between 1953 and 1966. In 1970 part of the hall was converted into a residential music college. A section of one of the wings was used as part of the museum's exhibition gallery. Since August the hall has been used for wedding receptions and conferences.

Of course, the centuries of history bound up in the hall have led to many stories. A male figure dressed in Victorian finery has been seen looking out of the window of the function room known as Eden Hall. A woman has been seen at the window of the bridal suite: she looks sad and lost – perhaps she is the deserted fiancée of Bobby Shafto. Numerous strange noises have been heard echoing through the hall, including the sound of footsteps when staff know they are alone. Certain rooms feel uncomfortable and workers are afraid to enter them alone. The spectre of an old lady is said

Beamish Hall before 1909 from an old picture postcard.

to haunt the Eden Bar; she is often seen after a social function and quite simply disappears when informed by the staff that it is time to leave.

Recently a visitor to the hall caught a dark apparition on camcorder. It detached itself from the shadows and joined a group of people wandering around the corridors, only to vanish after a matter of moments.

Otherworld North East's first investigation at the hall, on 12 March 2004, got underway by 10.40pm. The group split into two teams working in different parts of the hall so they wouldn't hear each other.

Beamish Hall, 2004.

In the oldest part of the building, on the ground floor, the team started to experience periods of unease, though neither EMF or temperature surveys picked up any anomalies. Initial attempts at pendulum dowsing gave no results, though at least one team member said that it felt as though the pendulum was being tugged. At 11pm dowsing picked up on a male spirit who worked at the hall in the time of the Shaftos. At the same time there was a 3.2°C drop in the temperature of the room. A digital dictaphone set up in an attempt to capture EVP gave no results.

In the room next door, the temperature fluctuated between 9 and 12°C though we could find no reason for this.

At 1.11pm, three team members heard movement on the floor above, and used the walkie-talkies to contact the other team to clarify their position. However the other team were in fact on the ground floor, on the opposite side of the building, but they could also hear the sound, and the temperature in their room dropped to 1°C. The source of the movement, which sounded like footsteps, remained a mystery.

The other team started work in the Monboucher Restaurant at 10.40pm. The team medium picked up on a man named Harold Ramsay, who apparently had suffered greatly from piles (which gave the medium an uncomfortable few minutes!). He described Ramsay as a ladies' man, who liked dancing and was visiting Beamish still looking for a woman named Ellen Coates. He'd wanted to marry her in 1941 but had left her behind when he went off to war.

Seven minutes later the medium saw a woman walk through the wall from reception. He described her as small with very long curling hair, wearing a figure-hugging dress. No EMF or temperature anomalies were detected, though when one of the team felt he was being watched from the dark corridor leading towards the kitchens, he took a photograph and caught a small light anomaly on camera.

From the restaurant, the group went to Shafto Hall and carried out EMF, photograph and temperature surveys. The room temperature averaged between 6-8°C. Almost immediately, the medium started picking up on a strong, angry spirit by the door to the kitchens, describing him as almost military in demeanour. When he asked the spirit to make a noise to show itself, the team heard a strange scraping sound that they couldn't identify.

The other team were still suffering temperature fluctuations, and were picking up a male spirit through dowsing. He claimed to have died at the hall as the result of an accident. Further along the corridor in the ground floor bar, a wind chime was set up as a trigger object. Dowsing indicated a spirit who was afraid

A light anomaly caught outside the Monboucher Restaurant.

of someone. At 11.30pm, a strange 'orb' light anomaly was caught on night-vision video in the corridor outside. Five minutes later, the battery in one of the camcorders drained, and it was decided to set up motion sensors on the bar.

At 11.30pm, the other group was upstairs in the bridal suite. The initial EMF sweep had produced no anomalies except the power cables in the walls and floor, but 15 minutes later an EMF anomaly appeared in the room between the bed and the wardrobe, at the height of around 5ft 5ins, and a reading also appeared on the bedpost. Soon, a reading appeared on the bed itself. The team could not explain these anomalies, no matter how hard they tried!

At 11.57am one of the team had his EMF meter switched off by something unseen. To switch off the meter you have to flick a switch! Fifteen minutes later, the team medium reported the strong presence of a woman in the room called Marion Lichfield. At this point, his surface body temperature was fluctuating between 7.8 and 28.1°C although he said he felt quite okay. He said that Marion's husband had been Franklin Lichfield, and that Marion had died on 17 June 1811 of what was probably colonic cancer. Apparently she had died in St. John's

Wood, London, but revisited Beamish as she had happy memories of the place.

Meanwhile, the other team were exploring the boiler rooms beneath the hall, where one team member was suffering an inexplicable feeling of sadness and another was feeling nauseous. No temperature or EMF anomalies were present, but strangely the compass the group was using refused to budge from pointing east! The group reported the constant feeling of being watched, but dowsing produced no results. At 1.20am, the team moved to the corridor and picked up a number of light anomalies dropping vertically through the air on night vision. There was also a very slight temperature variation. The team tried a back-to-back dowsing experiment, with two dowsers asking the same questions but unaware of their partner's response. Both dowsers got exactly the same results, that there was more than one spirit present and that one male in particular wished to communicate. While this was happening, the group's magnetic compass was swinging wildly, unable to settle on north.

On the first floor, the other group were having an interesting time in Eden Hall, where one of the investigators had been startled to see the silhouette of someone walk past the open door, only to find no-one there. One of the investigators said he could feel something in the room and walked across to the window, his body surface temperature fluctuating between 6.4-10°C as he did so. Standing in the window, the members of staff with the group said he was mimicking the posture of a spirit seen standing in that very same window, looking out across the grounds.

In the kitchens it was impossible to take a good EMF survey because of all the appliances in the room, but the atmosphere felt heavy and oppressive. Apparently many members

---

One investigator's eyewitness account

On my second visit to Beamish Hall I saw a powerful apparition that formed and faded for five minutes before vanishing. It was around 2am and we were having a break. Another team member asked me to go with him to a lobby he had a 'feeling' about. Arriving at the Shafto Hall lobby, by the kitchens, I could certainly smell roses and felt goosebumps on my spine! Glancing up the corridor we both saw the figure of a man standing by a wall ... it was more of an outline, but male-shaped. Though there were no features visible I felt he was watching us. I was glad not to be alone, as I might have doubted what I was seeing.

A couple of days later members of staff took a camcorder to that corridor and have footage of a man's shape.

I still haven't got a clue what it was!

---

of staff had reported feeling very uncomfortable in the kitchens, hearing crashes and bangs from the adjoining room. Right on cue the team started to hear a tapping sound they couldn't explain. The medium picked up on a male spirit named Max. Two of the female investigators started to feel very unwell, with tightness in their chests and wobbly legs. Quite suddenly, one of them felt as though she had been hit twice in the stomach. The team moved out of the kitchens to allow her to recover and the second team took their place. They moved to the Winter Gardens but heard noises, including a loud bang, coming from the kitchen. The female team members began to feel unwell, and when they moved back into the kitchen doorway, pendulum dowsing picked up on a male spirit who apparently meant to harm the group. One of the team reported feeling a cold pressure on her back. A minute later, both she and another team member suddenly started crying at the same time for no apparent reason.

After a short break, the group split up again at 4am, one team heading to the Brown Rooms while the other team went to the Eden Bar on the first floor.

The Eden Bar felt extremely cold, and everyone felt shivery: the air temperature was 4°C. Ten minutes into the vigil one of the investigators sat down and quite suddenly felt his knee go cold, describing the feeling almost as if a cat had jumped onto his lap. The area he was indicating was 6°C colder than the rest of his leg, and when one of the other investigators asked for another sign something was there, the EMF meter picked up a small signal that hadn't been present before.

In the Brown Rooms two of the investigators experienced temperature fluctuations and a number of bizarre light anomalies were caught on the night vision video. The investigators had challenged whatever was in the room to show itself. Rather rashly I offered to allow whatever was present

A strange light, taking an interest in one investigator, picked up on digital camera in the very active Brown Rooms.

to 'use my energy' then started to feel unwell and my surface body temperature dropped steadily from 11°C to 3°C. At that point a large 'orb' anomaly was caught on night vision, leaving my body and heading towards the cameraman, whereupon it arced around and disappeared through the opposite

In the Brown Rooms. Night vision video captures a light anomaly leaving my body and heading towards the cameraman.

wall. Four minutes later the atmosphere changed again, and the cameraman suddenly felt as though something had grabbed the temperature gun and was trying to wrestle it out of his hand … The gun was recording temperature fluctuations of around 20°C up and down and constantly shifting. The experience lasted two minutes before the cameraman was released, leaving him (and me) shaken and in urgent need of caffeine!

Other activity (that can possibly be explained) was the smell of lavender on the stairwells reported by many people, as well as a peculiar smell of burning on one landing. There were several cases of torch batteries being drained. At 5.30am, while sitting in the main office awaiting the return of the second team, investigators heard a door slamming outside in the lobby, followed by footsteps: no-one was there. The second group was still on the first floor and nowhere near the lobby.

On 7 May we returned with a larger team to cover more ground and revisit areas of known activity from the previous investigation as well as areas which hadn't been touched.

In Shafto Hall a couple of 'orb' light anomalies were caught on digital camera. At least one was actually seen by

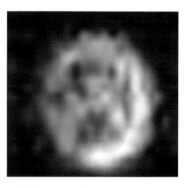

A light anomaly in Shafto Hall.

one of the investigators. Pendulum dowsing proved useless, but through the night everyone agreed that there was an oppressive, heavy atmosphere by the doors to the kitchen: at around 5am two members of the team sat and watched a partial apparition form and unform in that area for nearly five minutes. When one team member asked for a sign that there was a spirit in the hall, banging and crashing could be heard from the kitchens.

In the kitchens all four teams picked up a strong unpleasant male presence who perhaps meant them harm. Three of the groups got the name 'Max' through dowsing, and all four groups had team members suffer from chills and nausea. Several noises of movement, including clanging and banging, were heard from the kitchens, usually from the preparation area and there was the constant feeling of being watched. At one point there was a 5°C air temperature drop in just under

I was feeling distinctly unwell and very cold.

The kitchen, where the atmosphere was highly charged.

The Bridal Suite, where cameras refused to function properly.

three minutes. As an experiment, blue strobe lights were set up with a single investigator left to observe any effects: he reported feeling very unnerved and threatened. Ambient background EMF readings doubled during the period of the blue strobes, fading back to normal when they were switched off.

In the Monboucher Restaurant, things didn't seem as active as they'd been previously, with no temperature or EMF results. One investigator tried dowsing which indicated the presence of a male, aged 35, who had lived in the Hall in the 1900s and was happy there.

In the back rooms of the old quarter of the building, there were few results, with no EMF or temperature anomalies in the main suite of rooms, and the very weak dowsing result of a possible female spirit.

In the cellars below the ladies' toilets, the investigators had little luck until 12.30am, when dowsing indicated the presence of a spirit named Catherine Cedar, who had worked in the kitchens. The dowser's temperature fluctuated by 3°C. There was also an unidentifiable small reading on the EMF meter which vanished when the dowsing stopped. Footsteps were heard above, but on investigation no-one was present.

In the corridor on the first floor footsteps were heard in the adjoining Eden lounge, and then a lot of 'orb' anomalies caught on night vision camcorder – but only when the team asked for anything present to show itself.

The Bridal Suite once again confused and astounded the investigation team, with initial EMF and temperature sweeps picking up no anomalies. Suddenly there was a high EMF reading around the bed and a cold breeze from an untraceable source felt by a number of investigators. There were problems with cameras focusing, and creaking noises were heard from the corridor outside when people asked for a sign. At 12.46am, one of the team asked for a sign that someone was there; the EMF meter peaked suddenly at maximum, and a light was seen flashing across the wall. An hour later, no EMFs were registering until one of the team members sat on the bed and asked for anything present to join him. The EMF meter then picked up a high reading on the bed next to him, and the bed temperature was 3.5°C colder than the pillow, though they had previously been the same. One of the team heard something from the en-suite bathroom, and every time he took a flash photograph in there, there was the sound of banging from the corridor outside the bathroom wall. This was tried more than ten times, each time with a bang or scratching sounds accompanying the flash from the camera. Dowsing was attempted in the suite, but unfortunately the only result was that the spirit was female.

Vigils in the Brown Rooms started slowly with nothing more than a feeling of being watched. At 1.45am dowsing picked up on a man named Robert. One of the staff with the team reported that a little boy had spoken to a 'ghost' two weeks ago at a wedding in the hall. When asked the pendulum responded that this spirit was the one who had communicated with the boy. The spirit liked children, but wasn't happy at the prospect of the hall being changed around in the near future. The dowsing with 'Robert' was accompanied by minor temperature fluc-

tuations in both the dowser and the air, and footsteps were heard once again. In the Yellow rooms, a strange banging sound was heard in the corridor, while batteries from a torch began to drain. Two of the group reported feeling a strangle tingling sensation, as if the air was thick with electricity but no EMFs were detected. Soon afterwards, one of the toilet doors slammed shut; when we tried it we discovered it would have had to be closed with some force to make the same noise.

There seems little doubt after the two investigations at Beamish Hall that there is something very strange going on. We found a wide range of classic and fascinating phenomena. The Otherworld North East team hopes to be able to continue research there in future months.

Beamish Hall around 1900.

32. St Thomas' Eve

Crook Hall, near Durham

Crook Hall in near Durham is a medieval Manor House, originally built in the latter half of the 13th century on lands owned by Sydgate Manor. Early in the 14th century, the land passed to Peter de Croke, from whom the hall gained its name. The Great Hall and a screened passage remain from the medieval building. The passage now leads to a Jacobean addition. Near the passage are the haunted stairs – a peculiar set of wooden steps which head up to the ceiling and then stop. This route to the upper floors is now blocked.

It is said that on St Thomas' Eve, 20th December, a radiant woman, dressed completely in white, glides down the stairs. On other occasions she has been seen in the Jacobean room, which is where most visitors get a sense of her presence. Legend has it that she is the niece of Cuthbert Billingham, a man thought to be associated with the Hall in 1425, though of course why she would be haunting the Jacobean room is another matter entirely!

Crook Hall, mid-19th century,

33. A Store Room Cell

Durham Prison, Durham

A tale is told that in the winter of 1947, two occupants of a ground floor cell in the main wing of Durham Gaol took a violent dislike to each other, fighting and quarrelling all the time. Eventually one of the cellmates managed to sneak a kitchen knife into the cell, and next time they had an encounter he used it to make sure he won the argument, once and for all.

Unlike many such incidents, often reported as having 'no witnesses', this seems to have become one of the most witnessed crimes in the gaol's history. Many prisoners locked in this cell have found themselves watching a rerun of the tragedy in the

Durham gaol around 1900.

middle of the night, and were often found white-faced and shaking the following morning, and able to describe the crime vividly. It is said that the cell in question is now used exclusively for storage, so no-one knows whether the ghostly murder still replays over the long nights of the winter months.

34. The Red Room

Case Study 28 November 2003
The House, Middlesbrough

Ghost Haunted North East were called to The House, a town centre pub in Middlesbrough, on 28 November 2003 to investigate alleged poltergeist activity reported by staff who were feeling nervous about unexplained incidents. The episodes focused around the ground floor bar, where glasses and bottles had fallen mysteriously off their shelves when no-one was near, almost as if they'd been knocked or thrown, and strange footsteps had been heard crossing the bar. A threatening, shadowy figure had also been seen in the cellars. It was the top floor of the building that seemed to give rise to the greatest concern, with one room, the 'red room', making many of the staff very uncomfortable indeed. According to the manager of The House, someone had hanged themselves in this room.

The team talked to staff about the alleged activity, and discovered that at one point the 'red room' used to be rented out, but due to the strange occurrences that practice had stopped. Trigger objects such as crucifixes, lock-off cameras and magnetic compasses were set up, then the investigation began.

There had been reports of a ghostly figure seen in the ladies' toilets so a vigil was held there, though with few results. There was some erratic rod dowsing, but the rods weren't moving consistently enough to be classed as conclusive evidence.

The pool table area and the bar were uneventful at first, but later strong dowsing results indicated the presence of a

The back stairs, with a light anomaly above the camera – which proved to be only dust.

spirit, and at least four people heard running footsteps over the floor, though no-one was there. A pendulum was placed in a heavy portable metal clamp and put on the shelves behind the bar which bottles had 'jumped off'. When the clamp was checked later it seemed to have been knocked from its original position. A digital dictaphone was set up on one of the pool tables, but produced no results.

With so little activity the Ghost Haunted team decided to attempt a séance on the top floor, with the team medium looking on. The group asked anything present to show itself in some way. I was standing on the stairwell attempting pendulum dowsing and seemed to be getting a response to each question asked by the group in the séance – a constant 'no'.

After a couple of minutes, the dowsing responses stopped and the cameras recording the séance started to pick up strange moving 'orbs' or light anomalies zipping through the circle. Just on cue, as the presence was again asked for a sign, the motion sensor set up in the neighbouring red room was triggered. The three investigators who entered the room to switch off the sensors found nothing that could have triggered them, but each reported feeling a heavy static charge in the air that vanished as soon as they reached for EMF meters.

Most of the team returned to the séance, leaving a few people in the red room, with the medium standing in the doorway. Soon, one of the investigators in the red room began to feel ill, and his temperature started to fluctuate. The medium went into a trance, breathing in a very 'ragged' way as if he had something wrong with his chest. He didn't respond to his name being called or other external stimuli. As he was becoming distressed, we decided to take him outside. He suddenly said, 'He's got hold of me!' before we led him out. Later he told us that it had been a male spirit called Grainger, though environmental readings didn't find anything extraordinary at the time.

Three of the team, including myself, locked ourselves in the red room to see if anything would happen. We did elec-

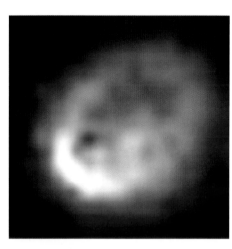

An anomaly caught on digital camera during the investigation.

tromagnetic and temperature surveys, took photographs and tried dowsing, but with little success. The room felt warm and comfortable, so more trigger objects were set up and we headed elsewhere.

Little more happened during the investigation. The medium picked up a number of names that the manager could confirm as being people associated with the pub's past. A team member also heard ragged breathing in the back stairwell of the pub, though he was alone at the time: later the medium did pick up the presence of a spirit there.

My night at The House was quite possibly the most interesting Friday night I've ever spent in Middlesbrough!

The notorious red room at The House.

35. Down in the Deep

Killhope Lead Mine, County Durham

The Killhope Lead Mines are in the heart of the North Pennines between Stanhope and Alston. They are now a visitor attraction. Visitors have access to the grounds and to the mines (and temporary loan of wellington boots, a hard hat and a headlamp!) Even at the height of of summer, Killhope can seem cold as it is situated at the giddy heights of 1,500 feet above sea level.

Park Level Mine opened in 1853 and operated until 1910. The famous ten-metre diameter waterwheel, now restored, was built in the 1870s to crush and separate lead ore from waste. The mine opened again briefly during the First World War to help supply the region's need for lead.

However, Park Level was not the first mine to explore the fourteen veins of rich lead ore at Killhope. Four Roman lead ingots have been found nearby. This could suggest local mining or perhaps simply trade. It is certain that the area provided lead through the medieval period, and evidence of Elizabethan tunnels were unearthed by the Park Level miners as they followed the veins of ore. These older tunnels were nicknamed 'Old Men of the Mines' and can easily be identified by the different cutting techniques in the walls.

In the 1980s, the area known as the 'washing floor' by the wheel was subject to a great deal of archaeological research. Here young boys, usually about eight or nine years old, worked long gruelling hours breaking apart the lead ore from the waste – on average for about fourpence a day! This work was taken over by the wheel when it was built in the 1870s, but not before the washer boys had been immortalised in a local song about child exploitation. Young boys were also

The lonely moors around Killhope photographed before restoration of the famous wheel.

employed in the mines to open and close doors, providing a constant through-draft of fresh air for the four-mile deep mineshafts.

Lives were lost through accidents in Park Level but the poor conditions, in particular the constant damp, claimed more victims from tuberculosis and similar conditions: the average miner was not expected to live into his forties. Many injuries were sustained due to the practice of packing drilled holes in the workface with volatile explosives – by hand. Miners would also work in near or complete darkness to save on pricey candles.

It's not surprising that there are ghost stories about Killhope and its mine, the museum building and even the ruined cottages in the outlying forests.

The first investigation at Killhope Lead Mines by a Prudhoe-based paranormal investigator proved to be more than a little scary. A woman was heard screaming in the forest during the night. When the team took shelter in one of the old miners' cottages the door rattled and shook as if someone was trying to get in: when they looked, no-one was there. Strange 'orb' lights were also caught on night vision video. On his second visit to the site, this time with Ghost Haunted North East, the spirit of a girl playing among the trees was picked up by the team medium. Apparently, the child was upset at the work going on at the mine site though why was never clarified. The medium also picked up on a lot of residual activity, or memories of the men, women and children who worked at the mines as well as a strong female presence. There was also, he said, the spirit of a young man who had died tragically; in fact there is a plaque on site to commemorate this event.

36. GHOSTLY JUSTICE

Lumley Mill, County Durham

One of the most popular ghost stories in County Durham during the 17th century was that of John Grahame and the Mill at Lumley. It is said that one night John Grahame was hard at work in the mill, and failed to notice that it had passed midnight. Quite suddenly, he felt the atmosphere in the mill change, and turned around to see a young woman in her twenties before him. Her dress was covered in blood from multiple head-wounds. The miller realised that no-one could be that injured and live.

Resisting the urge to run from the mill, the trembling Grahame asked the girl what she wanted. She said that she'd been murdered and her body thrown down a pit – her murderer was a collier named Mark Sharpe.

The girl had been working for Grahame's neighbour, John Walker, who had 'done her wrong' but had promised to look after her. Walker had sent her away with Sharpe 'to a place for proper care', but instead Sharpe had turned on her with a coal pick, striking her head until she was dead. He'd then concealed the murder weapon under a bank, hidden his bloodied clothes and shoes, and dumped her body in the mine. She told the terrified miller that if he didn't uncover the truth, she'd haunt him till the end of his days – and then vanished.

Needless to say, John Grahame shut the mill equipment down for the night and ran home to his wife to ponder the words of the grim spirit. Once safely at home he decided to put his experience down to a tired mind and an overactive imagination.

Weeks passed and the miller said nothing. It is said that he became a sombre man and refused to work late in the mill. One night he did stay a little later than usual, and on his way home through the woods was once again confronted by the ghost of the murdered girl. The miller fled but again decided not to say anything. Over the months that followed his health began to fail him and he became a shadow of the man he was.

That year, on St. Thomas's Eve, Grahame was in his garden when the dead girl appeared before him once more. The miller could no longer pretend that she was just a product of his imagination and finally agreed to bring her murderer to light. The following morning he went to the local magistrate with what he'd been told. Very soon, the mine was searched and the girl's decayed body was found; next, the magistrate followed Grahame's instructions and found the pick and Sharpe's discarded clothing.

Hours later John Walker and Mark Sharpe were arrested, and the story came to light. Walker had mistreated his wife, and after her death he'd taken in his young niece. She'd become pregnant, and though she never admitted who the father was, she'd understood that Walker would look after her. Shortly afterwards, she had disappeared.

The two men were tried for murder in 1631, found guilty and sentenced to death. Interestingly, it seems ghosts also played a part in the trial, one source reading '... One Mr. Fairhair, gave it in evidence, upon oath, that he saw the likeness of a child stand upon Walker's shoulders during the time of the trial; at which time the judge was very much troubled, and gave the sentence on the night...'

The mill at Lumley is no longer there, but the story is still told of the dead girl who helped to bring her murderer to justice.

37. Winter's Ghost

North Road Station, Darlington

The station was built in the 1840s to serve the Darlington to Stockton rail service. By 1890 it was already home to a ghostly apparition, that of a man named Winter who had committed suicide there and whose body had been stored in the cellars until it could be taken to the morgue. The first recorded sighting of the apparition was in December 1890, when the night-watchman saw a man coming out of an outbuilding dressed in a Victorian railway uniform with cap and coat, a black retriever at his heels. Thinking that this was an intruder, the night watchman threw a punch at the mysterious figure, but neither man nor dog took any notice of his presence. The watchman's knuckles made contact with nothing but the wall beyond. This was immediately reported to the Society of Psychic Research and taken as a serious sighting, especially after discovering that the night-watchman in question was a teetotaller.

North Road Station was closed in 1962 and the buildings fell derelict. In the early 1970s the place was turned into a railway museum but there are still occasional reports of a strange figure and a black dog.

38. BLACK CAT

The Oak Tree Inn, Tantobie

The Oak Tree Inn in Tantobie was once a small manor house, home to members of the Liddell family related to the Liddells of Ravensworth. Dating back to at least the turn of the 18th century, the building also seems to contain older medieval elements.

The inn is said to house many strange phenomena, from heavy thundering footsteps in the upper levels, to an apparition walking behind the bar or sitting by the fireplace warming himself. The seated figure has often been seen wearing a tricorn hat; sometimes he is seen enjoying a drink before vanishing in front of startled witnesses.

More worryingly, the ghost seems to have displayed poltergeist tendencies in the past, moving drinks around and playing with the gas supplies in the cellar. It also appears to have developed a sense of humour; the door to the gents' toilets seems to be held closed while the poor user attempts desperately to get out ... until the door suddenly flies open with no evidence of what was restraining it.

Bizarre as it seems, the inn's other long-standing ghost is that of a small black cat, often seen running around the bar, towards the kitchens, and sometimes out of the front door, only to vanish, quite literally, into thin air.

39. £5,000 BOUNTY

Redworth Hall Hotel

Redworth Hall dates back to 1693. It was home to the Crozier and Surtees families until the 1950s when it was sold to a hotel group. Today it is difficult to believe that Redworth was once known as one of the most haunted buildings in the north.

The phenomena range from disembodied cries to running footsteps. Cold spots and freezing breezes have been felt in a number of the bedrooms, and apparitions have been seen wandering the halls at night.

Phantom pipers play ghostly music. Doors were rattled, perhaps by the Grey Lady that is supposed to walk the halls. She is thought to be the spectre of a woman who threw herself from the tower; the tale is remarkably similar to that of the Pink Lady of Bamburgh! So strong were the feelings of being watched and followed that a bounty was placed on the ghosts' heads in 1990: £5,000 to the first person who could give solid proof that the hall was haunted. Sadly, no one succeeded in earning it before the offer expired.

40. IN A BIT OF A PICKLE

Sedgefield, County Durham

Local legend has it that there is a lost ancient tunnel leading from St. Edmund's Church to the rectory, and that it is haunted by the ghost of the 'Pickled Parson'. This rather angry spirit is said to be John Gamage, rector of Sedgefield in 1747. Just days before he was about to collect his tithe from the local farmers, he dropped dead from unknown cause. His wife, rather than giving him a speedy and proper burial, was determined that she would at least have one last year's tithes. Instead of telling people about Gamage's death, she stored him in salt until after the tithes had been paid, brushed him off and put him to bed and then told everybody that he had just died! But it seems that John Gamage was unhappy with his wife's actions, and haunted the rectory for many years, his hideous cries echoing through the night. Fortunately for the local populace, that part of the rectory burned down in 1792 – and the ghost of Gamage, driven from his usual haunt, took his woes to the lost tunnel where he is said still to roam and cry out in the night.

AFTERWORD

Compelling if bizarre photographs, and fascinating video footage, plus recorded inexplicable environmental changes such as temperature and electromagnetic fluctuations are evidence that the supernatural is most definitely out there – and sometimes making its presence felt!

After a year of investigating various sites across the North East and further afield, the Otherworld North East team seem to have found a great deal to indicate *something else* with us in our everyday lives.

It is up to the individual reader to decide whether or not our researches provide conclusive evidence of the paranormal; some people believe without question; others remain sceptical even in the face of evidence. But who can truly say who is right and who is wrong?

Otherworld North East will continue to search for rational explanations for the phenomena we record, concluding for the time being that there are undoubtedly more questions than answers surrounding the mysteries of the North East's haunted places …

… but this is nothing new …

James Pilkington, Bishop of Durham wrote to the Archbishop of Canterbury around 1565 concerning a local man who apparently conducted conversations with a ghost:

… says he has spoken with one of his neighbours that died four year since or more. Divers times he says he has seen him and talked with him, and took with him the curate, the schoolmaster, and other neighbours, which all affirm that they have seen him too. These things so common here, and none of authority that will gainsay it, but rather believe and confirm it, that everyone believes it. If I had known how to have examined with authority, I would have done it.

CONTACTS & SOURCES

Websites (correct at time of writing)

Official Otherworld North East Website
http://www.otherworldne.org.uk

TAPS (The Answers People Seek)
http://www.theanswerspeopleseek.com

UK Ghost Investigators
http://www.ukghostinvestigators.org.uk

The British Paranormal Alliance
http://www.paranormal-alliance.co.uk

Ghosts UK
http://www.ghosts-uk.net

Team Maynard
http://www.deanmaynard.com

Avalon Skies
http://www.avalon-skies.org

Ghost Haunted
http://www.ghosthaunted.co.uk

NEPUK (North East Paranormal UK)
http://www.nepuk.co.uk

Books and Journals

Balfour, M.C. *Printed Folk-lore Concerning Northumberland*, 1903

Bath, J. *Dancing with the Devil and other True Tales of Northern Witchcraft*, Tyne Bridge Publishing, 2002

Brand, J. *Observations on Popular Antiquities*, 1777

Forman, J. *Haunted Royal Homes*, 1987

Forster, E. *Weird Tales of Northumbria*, 1970

Hallam, J. *Ghosts of the North*, David and Charlies, 1976

Hardy, J. *Silky: A Northumbrian Tradition*, 1862

Harper, C.G. *Haunted Houses*, 1907

Histon, V. *Nightmare on Grey Street: Newcastle's Darker Side*, Tyne Bridge Publishing, 2000

Histon, V. *Ghosts of Grainger Town: Further tales from Newcastle's Darker Side*, Tyne Bridge Publishing, 2001

Jackson, C.C. (ed) *Bainbridge & Co. Ltd Chronicle 22nd October 1988*, 1988

Linahan, L. *The North of England Ghost Trail*, 1997

Newton, J. (ed) *Early Modern Ghosts*, University of Durham, 2002

Price, H. *Poltergeist: Tales of the Supernatural*, 1945

Redfern, B. *The Shadow of the Gallows*, Tyne Bridge Publishing, 2003

Spencer, J. & A. *The Ghost Handbook*, 1998

Spencer, J. & A. *The Encyclopedia of Ghosts and Spirits*, 1992

Tomlinson, W.W. *Denton Hall and its Associations*, 1894

Tynedale, M. *Legends and Folk Lore of Northumbria*, Collins' Clear Tyne Press, 1932

Underwood, P. *The A-Z of British Ghosts*, 1993

Underwood, P. *This Haunted Isle*, 1993

Warren, M. & Wells, T. *Ghosts of the North*, 1995